curious directive

Pioneer

T0347775

Bloomsbury Methuen Drama
An imprint of Bloomsbury Publishing Plc

B L O O M S B U R Y
LONDON • NEW DELHI • NEW YORK • SYDNEY

Bloomsbury Methuen Drama

An imprint of Bloomsbury Publishing Plc

50 Bedford Square
London
WC1B 3DP
UK

1385 Broadway
New York
NY 10018
USA

www.bloomsbury.com

BLOOMSBURY, METHUEN DRAMA and the Diana logo
are trademarks of Bloomsbury Publishing Plc

First published 2015

British Library Cataloguing-in-Publication Data
A catalogue record for this book is available from the British Library

ISBN: PB: 978-1-4742-5592-9
ePub: 978-1-4742-5593-6
ePDF: 978-1-4742-5594-3

Library of Congress Cataloging-in-Publication Data
A catalog record for this book is available from the Library of Congress

Typeset by Country Setting, Kingsdown, Kent CT14 8ES

Pioneer

For anyone who has ever set sail in search of new worlds.

*For anyone who has made it possible for
their fellow humans do so.*

For anyone who has been left behind.

You are our inspiration. You are the wind in our sails.

Thank you.

Introduction

The discussion which sparked *Pioneer* took place in a room just off the cavernous corridors of the Natural History Museum, London, in November 2012. But I encountered this 'Nature Live' discussion completely by chance.

I was rushing up the steps of the museum, aware of being late for an installation that was part of their Friday night 'Lates' series. Inside Hintze Hall where 'Dippy' the diplodocus calls home, I overheard someone talking about a web discussion with the founder of a Mars mission. As they walked away, I decided to follow. All three of us arrived at a huge closed door. They were clearly late. Having abandoned the installation I originally set out to see, I crept in alongside these two strangers. Inside a Skype discussion was taking place with the Dutch entrepreneur Bas Lansdorp, CEO of 'Mars One'. I had essentially gate-crashed a talk, but no one seemed to mind. As I watched a heated debate unravel, I took notes on a napkin.

The audience were clearly divided about this mission to Mars, which proposed to fund itself by selling the media rights to what is often (perhaps reductively) described as 'Big Brother in space.'

Some called out that the motivations of the 'Mars One' mission were 'deliberately sensationalist'. Others fought back with 'the deep originality of the idea'. For those readers who haven't heard of 'Mars One', I suggest visiting mars-one.org at some point. It's a fascinating premise.

After the discussion I remember sitting on a stool, completely stunned. I remember texting my long-time collaborator, Russell Woodhead, 'Rus – just found the source of a curious directive show. Mars. Why, how, when? More soon.'

The planned 'Mars One' mission sits nestled inside the genesis of what *Pioneer* was to become. But when we began to research the science underpinning the mission, we soon unearthed various flaws in their proposed plans. This is not to say that we look down on the 'Mars One' mission from a pedestal of scepticism. Quite the opposite. For us, 'Mars One' represents the single most successful re-ignition of interest in human space travel since the original US/Soviet space race in the 1960s. Whatever happens now, sociologically 'Mars One' has succeeded.

From 2015 onwards, we are entering a brave new era for space travel. Some of the greatest business minds in modern history are interested in investing. And so naturally, as a company which explores the implications of science on the present day, we were drawn to respond with a play. To imagine a future where something has progressed. A future in fact where a mission has already been attempted, and failed. Our play begins in 2029.

Our process started in a barn in Norfolk in March 2014, where we were surrounded by nature: fields, woodland and the North Sea. For a play about Mars, such a place may seem like an odd choice. But as with many creative processes, often being around the antithesis of what you are trying to re-create/extract/reconfigure, can lead to profoundly shifting and original insights. Our process explored a reconnection with nature. Much of our sound and video design in the production of *Pioneer* emerged from these surroundings. And our storyboard for this complicated interwoven piece arrived from this simple reconnection with nature.

We wanted to make an empowering piece of theatre. So *Pioneer* is partly an imperative. We started immersing ourselves in the sci-fi geniuses of the past; Asimov, Arthur C. Clarke, Philip K. Dick, Ray Bradbury and others. We wanted to make small statements about how we see the world in the future. A world where women take leading roles in science, but a world where this is just how it is, rather than a statement about gender politics in the workplace. *Pioneer* would still be populated by the same characters we think of when we say 'science fiction'. But we were really creating a 'science fact' play. We laid out three narratives. Firstly, Shari and Rudi's two incredible minds inside mission control with their gruelling schedules, the whispering corridors and the knife-edge decisions which need to be made. Secondly, those leading the science exploration on Mars, Imke and Oskar: those on their way or on Mars. Thirdly, a narrative about the 'everypeople' of Ivan and Alyosha, people like me and you reading perhaps. People who don't understand all the science but nonetheless feel the importance of what is happening as we aim to land humans on another planet.

We looked back in time too; to the first seafarers who set out 'scared shitless of dragons and sirens ans tsunamis' all the way back to that moment represented in the book of Genesis, when Eve wondered 'why'? when she questioned. We were keen to reframe what was happening when Adam and Eve were 'exiled' from Eden by God. We wanted to explore what happens if we judged Eve as being curious about the world by picking that apple. In the face of the apparent 'fall from grace', was she really jumping into the darkness, jumping into an unknown space?

Debate and conflict is at the heart of what we think makes an extraordinary story. We brought our own experiences of the eternal question 'Are we alone?' into the devising room. And it seems that space-travel conversations have sparked over Christmas dinners, in taxis, pubs and in the freezing cold waiting at bus stops.

This particular human remembers walking home in Norfolk along a country road, right by the sea, looking up at the sky and arguing with a close friend about why interplanetary space travel is possible and important. We had almost diametrically opposing opinions. It was a heated debate. The other side being: let's sort out our problems here first. This debate took place under the silent, infinite backdrop of the hundreds of millions of stars which gently 'domed' around us, like a giant snow globe. This discussion has stayed with me. It made me realise that not everyone shares my philosophy of space travel. But also that binary relationships are important.

Boss and assistant, sisters, brothers. These are in *Pioneer*. We see Mars as a sibling of Earth. Somewhere we hope to get closer to at some point.

People are at the heart of a great science fiction play. That's what we hope we've achieved.

It has been a profound experience exploring interplanetary travel.

Our conclusions exist within the grey areas, within the middle ground. They reflect the complexity of the behaviour of humans when faced with history-changing decisions.

I'm sure we'll return to the elegant themes of astrobiology and astrophysics in the future.

Perhaps when we're a little older.

A huge number of people were involved in *Pioneer*. In small and enormous ways. They know who they are. And they have been part of the ancient pastime of looking up at the night sky and hoping to find answers.

Jack Lowe
Artistic Director, curious directive

Special thanks

The creative associates of curious directive (Adam Alston, Jasmine Robinson, Karina Sugden, Gareth Taylor, Jo Walker, and Russell Woodhead).

Diana Lowe and David Adlard, Shelagh Cook (Spixworth Hall Barns), Old Vic New Voices, Corton House Elderly Care Home, Norfolk and Norwich Festival, Watford Palace Theatre, Anthony Roberts and his team at Escalator East to Edinburgh, Norfolk County Council Arts Team, Norwich Arts Centre, Paines Plough, English Touring Theatre, Cambridge Junction, The Thanet, Southwark Playhouse and Arts Council England.

DR. LEWIS DARTNELL (astrobiologist) for helping to sculpt our characters with sugar sachets and for introducing us to the concept of 'competence porn' when writing dialogue.

CHRIS THORPE for picking up the phone to talk through the story. For his incessant and selfless desire to help out younger artists.

JAMES MACKENZIE (programmer of Zoo Venues, Edinburgh) for saying 'yes' before a word or image was confirmed.

BRIGID LARMOUR (and her team at Watford Palace Theatre) for their constant encouragement throughout 2014.

CAROLINE RICHARDSON (from Norwich Playhouse) for her surprising note on the dramaturgy of 'arrows'.

WILLIAM GALLINSKY (from Norfolk and Norwich Festival) and Alex Derbyshire for saying 'yes', very few questions asked.

The UK venues who have invited us to present the show under your roofs. We're very excited to be sharing the work with you.

Above: Character relationships mapped out on a pub table.
Below: Devising in Spixworth Barns, Norfolk, day 1.

Above: The photo which gave us the idea for Maartje's character.

Below: An early CAD print-out of the *Pioneer* design.

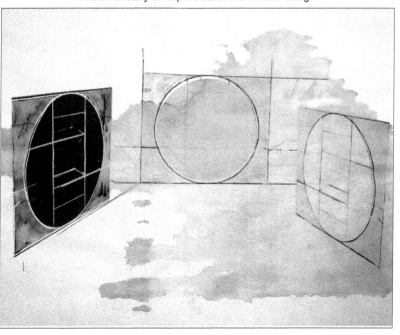

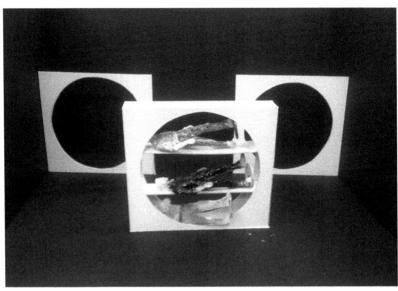

Above: An example of the white card design.

Below: The 'costs' in Imke's emotional arc.

Imke

- Family death (family)
- Sacrifice Maaije / Maaije's happiness
- EARTH
- Privacy (psychological)
- Sanity ... present
- Her life → not expecting to come back.
- Unwilling (not been to another planet)
- Normality.

Examples

ives in the

Unsaid

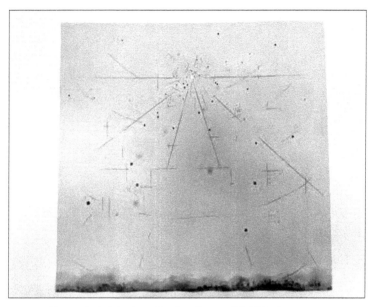

Above: A sketch of our Dutch galleon sail (which also acts as an infinity wall and floor cloth).

Below: Diagram depicting the journey of 'a day in the life of Imke on Mars'.

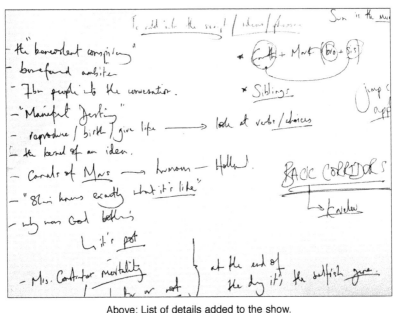

Above: List of details added to the show.

Below: Some notes about camera work in *Pioneer*.

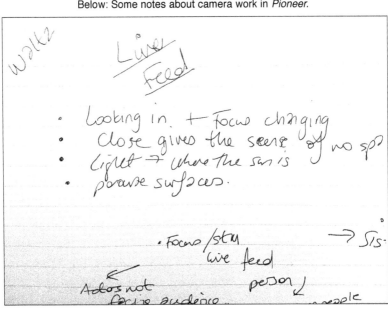

Notes

The performance space was originally designed to give the audience a 'widescreen' view.

The experience of watching *Pioneer* should therefore take into account the idea of being able to see simultaneous, fully formed stage pictures at the same time. This allows for layered storytelling.

However the production looks, the audience should be led visually by fluid, rhythmic storytelling with the use of stripped back, elegant design features.

The playing space is a large white canvas, eleven metres wide and eight metres deep.

At the upstage end, the canvas rises up to give the impression of an infinity curve.

At the downstage edge of the canvas there are tide-water markings and a wooden pole which holds the canvas in place.

The canvas represents a swooping sail of a Dutch galleon.

The white canvas has a series of line drawings and markings. These run from downstage to upstage, angled in towards upstage centre. This gives the floor a sense of perspective and distance.

There are also various painted circles on the floor which gradually become smaller from downstage to upstage centre. This again gives the floor a sense of perspective.

On the canvas are three large structures which we call 'portals'. Square in shape, these three portals have a large circular hole cut through the middle, creating three circular 'portals.' Each side of the portal has a blind, which is operated manually using a pulley. The blinds also act as projection surfaces during the play.

All three portals, although large objects, are trucked and therefore can glide across the canvas.

All other set pieces in this production were on trucks, including chairs, workstations and tables. This gives a sense that every object in the playing space has the potential to move.

At the opening of the play, the three portals are in a triangular formation on the canvas. This gives the impression that some sort of strange, white monolith has landed on the canvas.

Pioneer devising company

Stephen Bisland, Jesse Briton, David Burnett, Flora Denman, James Hardy, Rob Heaps, Susan Hingley, Caitlin Ince, Naveed Khan, Gabrielle Lombardo, Emily Lloyd-Saini, Avita Jay and Dudley Rees.

Direction Jack Lowe
Design Cecilia Carey
Video Jasmine Robinson
Sound Jo Walker
Light Joshua Pharo
Props Hannah Wales
Co-composition Adam Alston and Jo Walker
Stage Manager Jade Hunter
Production Manager Rhys Thomas
Technical Tour Managers Darrell Kirkbirde and Oliver Levett
Project Producer (tour 2015) Sarah Stribley
Assistant Director (tour 2015) Dan Hutton
Company General Manager (2014) Harriet Usher

Characters

Shari Dasgupta, *early thirties, Indian-born Flight Director of the Ghara missions*

Alyosha Korolev, *early twenties, a Russian astro-physicist PhD candidate*

Ivan Korolev, *late twenties, Alyosha's older brother*

Rudi Van Der Waal, *early thirties, Mission Operations Director of the Ghara missions*

Maartje Van der Berg, *late twenties, a Dutch-born marine biologist*

Imke Van der Berg, *early twenties, a Dutch-born botanist, younger sister of Maartje*

Oskar Dreschler, *mid-twenties, a Dutch-born biomechanical engineer, husband to Imke*

Stage grammar

Any stage direction steering an actor as to how to play a line is there as a guide, not set in stone.

A forward slash (/) depicts an active silence.

Beat depicts an inactive silence.

A dash (−) depicts an interruption.

An ellipsis (. . .) depicts a trailing off of a thought.

Part One

Preshow

As the audience enter the auditorium there is an atmosphere of quiet concentration.

'Abendleid' by Josef Rheinberger is playing followed by 'Bogoroditse Devo' by Gaudeamus.

In the downstage left corner, **Shari** is sitting on a wheelie chair at her small workstation. A lamp gently picks up her face in the darkness, as she types away. She is focused on this.

She is typing up her thoughts on the psychological preparations for the forthcoming Mars mission. The music relaxes her.

Alyosha, dressed in outdoor winter clothing, is crouched, observing her work. She cannot see him. **Shari** is in the space of **Alyosha**'s imagination.

Downstage right, **Ivan**, also in winter clothing, is crouched over a large model box simulation of the Martian landscape.

The model box has the red sand of Mars as well as various miniature 'habitation' modules.

Ivan uses an Anglepoise lamp to control the light cast over the model box.

Scene One

On clearance, the music swells and the light grows bright and tight vertically above **Shari**.

She looks up, as if accepting the light, expecting it.

We see **Rudi** enter and glide her backwards and out of focus.

Alyosha rises and crosses to **Ivan** stage right.

We follow the focus of the storytelling of **Ivan** *and* **Alyosha**.

Ivan *encourages* **Alyosha** *to begin.*

They turn to take in the audience.

Ivan *slowly begins to move the landscape (which is on trucks) from stage right to stage left. Fully focussed on the Martian landscape.*

A new piece of music begins. This is an underscore for **Alyosha** *giving an extract from his PhD on 'The Philosophy of Space Travel' at the Massachusetts Institute of Technology (MIT).*

Alyosha *looks to the audience, slowly follows the landscape and . . .*

Alyosha   As our solar system was formed there was a moment when the planets clicked into a cosmic procession around the sun.

In this moment Earth and Mars began a particular type of relationship together. A relationship based upon an ever-changing distance from one another. At her closest, she is fifty-six million kilometres away. At her furthest, four hundred and one million kilometres.

The landscape continues to glide from stage right to stage left. The **Brothers** *are lit in a gentle, horizontal corridor of light.*

Alyosha   So what keeps us connected to our next home? Our hearts? Our great scientific minds? Our great communicators and philosophers?

Or our ability to go there?

And as we weave a thread backwards and forwards through the future, our relationship will strengthen.

But in that first moment, what are we doing?

Are we playing God?

The landscape arrives downstage left. During this section, we begin to layer the action. The portal in the centre of the space begins to glow.

Behind a gauze it reveals **Imke***, lying on the middle bunk doing ten to twenty sit-ups.*

Ivan *moves around and gradually raises the blind to reveal* **Imke** *clearly lying on the bunk.*

Alyosha   When God formed a man out of the dust of the ground . . . what was he trying to do?

What was it about the dust which drew God in?

He picks up one of the habitation modules and inspects it. It becomes clear that **Imke** *is inside one of these modules on Mars.*

Alyosha   In many faiths, the story goes that God was creating a certain type of paradise.

But what was Eden?

Adam and Eve lived in a simulation, nothing more.

God created an enclosed area and planted a tree.

He planted a seed and waited for human nature to bloom.

But Eve. Eve wondered why? She questioned.

And when she saw that she was naked, the paradise was broken . . . but not lost.

Eve sacrificed herself because she wanted more. She sensed there was surely more to discover. Breaking free, defying restrictions, risking everything and jumping into the darkness.

Looking up and out at the darkness of the audience

It is this darkness where recklessness, where curiosity, where heroism can blossom. This is why humans have survived. This is why we must find a way to call other planets our home.

Transition

Ivan *talks assertively to the audience. This is their story. This is the beginning of what they knew.*

Ivan Imke and Oskar, a young Dutch couple, have been on Mars for 529 sols.

Alyosha Their AI helper, Jun –

Ivan – which stands for *Jinkou* (Human) *Uchyuu* (Space) *Nouryoku* (Intelligence) and was developed by the Japanese.

Alyosha Jun is one of the most advanced AI systems ever invented.

Scene Two
IMKE AND JUN I

Imke *and* **Jun** *are in the sleeping quarters of a 'Habitable Module' on Mars.*

Jun *is a handheld 'GoPro' camera mounted into a specially designed hand-held hemispherical structure.* **Jun** *moves freely and is puppeteered by an actor. The voice is spoken through a microphone.*

During all **Jun** *scenes we see a real-time live-feed of the action projected through* **Jun**-*cam.*

Imke *is wiping the sweat from her neck and is rolling deodorant on to her armpits.*

Imke *and* **Jun**'*s theme music begins. The sound of the Martian landscape can be heard in the distance.*

Jun *watches* **Imke** *as she sits on the bottom bunk.*

Jun It's early, Imke. You're not due to begin your day for another seventeen minutes. You really should go back to your bunk and rest. Your body needs 7.2 hours –

Imke I can't, I feel like I have a fever. Can you take my temperature, Jun?

Jun *does so.*

Imke Where's Oskar?

Jun   Oskar woke at four a.m., kissed you on the forehead and is currently recalibrating the communications transmitter.

Imke   Cold air please, Jun.

Jun   Would you like some water?

/

Imke   I had a bizarre dream.

Jun   Yes, I can see your sleep patterns were irregular around three a.m.

Imke *is putting on her red boiler suit.*

Imke   I dreamt I was lying on the grass in my garden on Earth. Oskar and I were looking up at the clouds making different shapes. And there was birdsong, summer air, people laughing in the next-door garden. And suddenly it was if someone hit a mute button. It went completely silent and . . . from the sky, dead flowers and plants started falling. At first small ones, and then more and more raining down on us until we were swimming in different dying roots and stems and petals. And the sound came back like a bomb exploding and I was trying to keep afloat . . . struggling to breathe as this river of flowers burst out of the garden and down the canals. I was swallowing the flowers, drowning in them and then . . . well . . . then I woke up.

Jun *comforting* **Imke**.

The central portal begins to move upstage, leaving **Imke** *and* **Jun** *in a much larger playing space.*

Jun   During sleep, your brain is trying to hold on to memories of Earth. This is natural, Imke. Oskar will tell you the same. It's healthy to hydrate before sleep and also –

Imke   You're right – prepare my suit. Oh, and make sure the O^2 vents are at 80 per cent today . . . and help me to keep the UV levels consistent in the nursery.

Jun   OK, Imke.

Imke   Are we speaking to Shari today?

Jun   Not today, Imke.

Imke *and* **Jun** *exit off the canvas stage right.*

Transition

Shari *enters into her workstation sitting on her wheelie chair.*

She is in slow motion.

It is the same set-up as the pre-show.

Alyosha *and* **Ivan** *appear from behind the portal.*

Their focus drifts to stage left.

Alyosha   This is Shari Dasgupta. One of the greatest minds in interplanetary space exploration.

Ivan   Flight director for the Ghara I mission.

Alyosha   A multi-billion dollar organisation now led by an elderly Indian widow named Mrs Singh.

Ivan   Shari is about to speak at a press conference watched by two billion people. The Ghara I mission is about to launch.

Alyosha   But, for now, she talks to her father. Over a thousand miles away in rural India.

Scene Three
SHARI TALKS TO THE WORLD

Shari *breaks out of her slow motion and speaks fluently to her father in Hindi on a video telephone. Her thoughts are projected as surtitles on to the stage-right and stage-left portal screens.*

The **Brothers** *stand either side of her, watching her conversation.*

She is having a brilliant time talking to her father.

The scene is played out at lightning pace.

Shari *Nahi meh tumko haath se ishaara nahi kar sakti hoo papa.*
[No I can't give you a wave, Papa.]

Ha, mujhe jaana parega. [Yes, I have to go.]

Ha, meh surdiyon meh ah rahi hoo. [Yes, I am coming to visit you
in the winter.]

Ha, meh teen minute meh live awongi. [Yes. I go live in three
minutes.]

We see **Rudi** *walk in from downstage right along the corridor, with a
Perspex screen in his hand.*

He walks efficiently with purpose.

Shari *Do urab log. Sab log kahte hai.* [Two billion people.
That's what they tell me.]

Ha. Meh etwaar ko phone karoongi. [Yes, I'll call you on Sunday.]

Nahi meh bhooli nahi. Meh bhi toomko pyar kurti hoo. [No, I haven't
forgotten. Love you too.]

Rudi *arrives, slightly interrupting. She hangs up.*

Rudi Rudi van der Waal.

Shari Where's Nikolai?

Rudi He's sick. I'm his assistant.

Lights change, in slow motion, **Shari** *and* **Rudi** *shake hands as the*
Brothers *fill the audience in.*

Ivan Rudi is young and ambitious.

Alyosha A graduate of the California Institute of Technology,
he worked at JPL –

Ivan – Jet Propulsion Laboratory –

Alyosha – and went on to become the first Westerner to
work within the Chinese Space Agency at the age of twenty-
three.

Ivan   This is only his third day at Ghara mission control.

Out of slow motion, lights change back.

Shari   Right.

Rudi   How do you feel?

Shari   I'm actually OK.

Rudi   You look nervous. You have a nervous face on. Water?

Shari   I don't have a nervous face. This is my normal face.

Rudi   Mrs Singh is delighted. Launching six months early is an incredible achievement.

Shari   You spoke to her?

Rudi   She just called from the hospital.

Shari   I thought she was too sick to talk.

Rudi   She tried to call you, it was engaged, so called Nikolai's office instead. She asked me to pass on that she's very proud that you're reading out her statement. Are you using in-ear, autocue or memory?

Shari   Just paper!

Rudi   Oh, and she had this sent through too.

He hands over a tube containing a picture.

Shari   What is it?

Rudi   It's a present. To commemorate the launch.

Shari   OK.

*She places it on her workstation and follows **Rudi** out of and down the corridor towards the press conference.*

Rudi   So. We'll take three questions after the launch. *New York Times*, *Cape Town Times*, and ending with *Le Monde*. You've read the releases?

Shari   Er . . . yes.

Rudi   Madam. If you haven't read them you need to tell me.

Shari   No, I have – I've just been distracted.

Rudi   OK. We'll go over them now. From the top?

Lights change. **Shari** *and* **Rudi** *continue in slow motion, The* **Brothers** *fill the audience in.*

Alyosha   Shari is known for her diplomatic temperament.

Ivan   She has a high level of perspicacity.

The ability to spot important details amongst a barrage of information.

But in this moment in her life, she is uneasy.

We never met Shari. We're speculating. This woman is a vital figure in the back corridors of our story.

Out of slow motion, lights change back.

Shari   Great. From the top.

Rudi   *New York Times* – Moira Sanchez is going to ask –

Lights change. **Shari** *and* **Rudi** *continue in slow motion, The* **Brothers** *play the journalists.*

Moira   – What are the safeguards against another mission failure like Mars One?

Out of slow motion, lights change back.

Shari   Seriously?

Rudi   Yeah – you know what she's like.

Shari   I've spoken about this at length. The Ghara mission is a completely different –

Rudi   – Don't open with that.

Shari   It's ridiculous they're still making comparisons.

Rudi   Madam, you're related to the Mars One mission failure.

Shari   Interruption. Mission interruption.

Rudi   Try to leave your past at the door today. All they want to hear from you is –

Shari   – OK. The advances in understanding we've gathered since the Mars One mission –

Rudi *is nodding.*

Shari   Why are you nodding?

Rudi   I'm encouraging. Make sure you mention the extensive tests to reduce human error to .1 per cent. Perhaps start by acknowledging the bravery of the Mars One team?

Shari   OK. The *Cape Town Times*?

Lights change. **Shari** *and* **Rudi** *continue in slow motion, The* **Brothers** *play the journalists.*

Jaan   You picked an American couple for Ghara along with a Frenchman. Can you explain your motivations for that?

Out of slow motion, lights change back.

Shari   Extensive tests since Mars One –

Rudi   – that's good.

Shari   Extensive tests have shown that a strong emotional connection between astronauts is vital to psychological survival on a mission of this length.

Rudi   Journey –

Shari   – journey of this length. Shared historical memories as well as the opportunity to form new ones together is most prominent in siblings and couples. Gregory and Rose are both world-class scientists and the Frenchman has three Michelin stars. Ha!

Rudi *laughs nervously.*

Rudi   Say Jean-Luc like the others is an extraordinary fighter pilot. And use your response to concede that Mars One should have had scientists on board rather than applicants from non-scientific backgrounds.

Shari   You just said move on from Mars One.

Rudi   Not if it helps you explain why Ghara One is born from science rather than . . . well, rather than the media circus of Mars One.

Shari   *Le Monde?*

Lights change. **Shari** *and* **Rudi** *continue in slow motion, the* **Brothers** *play the journalists.*

Jean-Pierre   There are various academics wanting to engage in the ethical debate of colonising Mars. There has been a controversy surrounding Ghara One and the distinct lack of a forum for these discussions.

Out of slow motion, lights change back.

Shari   When are we announcing the forum?

Rudi   Next week.

Shari   So what do I say to that?

Rudi   Say we're announcing a forum next week.

Shari   OK.

Rudi   One final thing. Make sure you mention the live broadcasts.

Shari   Really?

Rudi   I know Mars One really messed it up. I know. But you can't deny people are excited about this. So we had to be open to it.

Shari   Who's leading on that again?

Rudi   Channel 4, a British company, have the English-language rights.

Shari   Right. Yes, I knew that. Sorry. I've been distracted –

Rudi   – Just make sure you read her thoughts clearly and answer the questions accordingly. And enjoy yourself, madam.

Shari *rotates on the spot and suddenly she is centre stage in the press conference.*

Subtle sounds of phones, cameras clicking can be heard.

Two billion people are watching.

An autocue with **Shari***'s words is projected in the background.*

On the stage-right and stage-left portals we see a view of the luscious green island and the launch pad.

The audience are here to view the launch of Ghara One.

Shari   Good morning, everyone. And welcome to Sriharikota Island.

I imagine you were hoping Mrs Singh would be well enough to be with us at mission control for the launch.

She was sadly unable to travel from Mumbai.

Although I know she is often reluctant to admit it, she is an elderly woman now.

In her absence, she has asked me to read out some words to you all on this very special day.

She looks at the speech on the paper, takes a moment and then begins.

Her theme music begins.

The video design gradually drifts into the history of humans in space. We see countless images blending one into another.

Last Sunday, I sat in my chair in the corner of my hospital room.

I was looking up through my skylight at a beautiful square of blueness.

I was thinking about how humanity has felt great pride and loss in our quest to explore our solar system.

I myself have a strange role in this story.

Beat.

My great love in life has been architecture.

It has been said that architecture is the most political of the arts. My personal journey through it has been long. From our early work developing some of the poorest slums of India into habitable, beautiful environments, to the opening of our space hotels in lower earth orbit.

But it began as a small architecture firm in the early 1970s.

I was a woman of fifteen when I watched the Americans land on the Moon on a small black-and-white TV in my father's surgery.

And I wanted to be part of it.

Whatever it was.

I wondered whether one day I would be able to contribute to our progression into space.

But . . . after the opening of our space hotels, I realised perhaps that was *not* my one giant leap. I sat on my rocking chair in Pondicherry and I wondered, 'What will be next for me?'

In the spring of 2025 we all witnessed the baffling disappearance of the first human mission to Mars . . . an event which I'm sure will remain a 'Where were you when . . . ?' moment.

In the background we see the Ghara One astronauts begins their ascent to the shuttle.

Not just because of what we saw and those famous final words but . . . but because the tragedy of that mission might well have marked the end of our exploration to the red planet.

I wanted to help.

With the support of 128 private sponsors from thirty-seven different countries this is the most ambitious internationally funded space mission ever attempted.

But on Mars there will be no flags. We have no political agenda.

My nurses tell me I must keep a steady pulse, to not get too excited over the next six months if I am to live long enough to see the landings and the first steps of our Martians.

If I'm honest with you, my true hope was to go there myself, to retire and maybe live out my final days watching the purple sunsets.

Technologically, psychologically, physiologically and sociologically, we are prepared.

Ghara One will house and protect a biomechanical engineer, a medic and a computer scientist.

All astronauts are in position and carry on the movement sequence.

Bringing together the great sciences of old and new.

These three astronauts are on their way to the Ghara One rocket, ready to leave our planet for ever.

Beat.

The Earth is a beautiful place and our primary home . . . demarcated into continents, countries, districts, cities, towns, villages and home.

But be it alone, with a loved one or a group of friends, in a field, on a beach or at the top of skyscraper, we have all stared up at the stars and desperately tried to put into words what it is that we are feeling.

This mission is an articulation of that wonder.

It is our willingness to say: we will go there. Together.

The video ends and returns to a view of the rockets.

Thank you all.

Shari *leaves.* **Rudi** *reads in to his microphone.*

Rudi   Ms Dasgupta will be taking your questions after the launch.

Ladies and gentlemen, please put on your safety glasses and stand by.

He counts down in Hindi. The video grows into three large rocket boosters.

Primary Ignition:

10, 9, 8, 7, 6, 5, 4, 3, 2,1 . . .

Projected on to the walls of the space is:

FIVE MONTHS (*on stage right*).

THREE WEEKS (*on centre stage*).

AND TWO DAYS LATER (*on stage left*).

FIVE DAYS UNTIL THE MARS LANDINGS (*on all three*).

MOSCOW, RUSSIA, 3:05 A.M (*on centre stage*).

The sound of the launch swirls and blasts through the space.

We see the **Brothers** *come through the centre-stage portal as the stage-right and stage-left portals close in.*

We see that the **Brothers** *are dancing a waltz together.*

Part Two

Scene Four
AT THE BASE OF THE KREMLIN WALL

Moscow, Russia, 3:05 a.m., 1 January 2029.

Ivan *is on* **Alyosha**'s *back.*

Ivan *is humming a Richard Strauss Waltz with his brother,* **Alyosha**, *in a headlock.*

Ivan *has a bottle of vodka.*

They scuffle for a bit and then **Alyosha** *breaks free.*

Alyosha *kneels by the wall with a lighter.*

Ivan   Can you see his name?

Alyosha   . . . Gorbachev?

Ivan   You moron, that's politicians . . . you need Gagarin. He's above Gagarin.

Alyosha   Keep your voice down, Ivan.

Ivan   They categorise them. He's over there, I think.

/

Ivan   Hey, what is this?

Alyosha   It's my lighter.

Ivan   You smoking?

Alyosha   No, no –

Ivan   – You know how I fucking feel about smoking.

Alyosha   I'm not smoking OK, it's for marijuana.

Ivan   Marijuana?

Alyosha   Yeeeaah.

/

Ivan   That's OK.

Alyosha *goes back to searching.*

Alyosha (*whispering*)   Hey hey – there he is. Our great grandfather, Sergei.

Ivan   That's our name.

Alyosha   That's our name, there.

They laugh.

It's too much.

Ivan   It's like coolest graffiti in the world.

Alyosha *reaches over for drink.*

Alyosha   You think we'd be going to Mars if it wasn't for him?

Ivan   A lot to live up to. The whole space programme came from him. One man.

Alyosha   Fuck.

Ivan   What is her name again? The one in the Ghara mission. Rosie?

Alyosha   What?

Ivan   Rosalind.

Alyosha   Don't. Can't you fucking say her name right?

Ivan   Oh, Alyosha . . . why you sensitive?

Alyosha   Rose. Her name is Rose.

Ivan   You like them Yanky. You like to deflower the prom queen.

Alyosha   Superb, Ivan.

Ivan   What? You're telling me you're not getting fellated every night by some twenty-one-year-old cheerleader in your little dormitory in M.F.T.

Alyosha   M.I.T.

Ivan   I knew you had high standards but this . . . this is really high. You think you'd get past her husband Gregory with your tiny fists and tiny penis.

Alyosha   Tiny penis! (*As if* **Ivan** *is an idiot.*)

Ivan   Besides, there's no privacy on those missions.

Alyosha   Ivan. I take an interest in the great moments in our lifetime and you're making penis jokes. I should be on the next flight back to the States.

Ivan   Ah, that's right, college boy, you'll be working for a hedge fund in six months. Spreading your legs in front of spreadsheets.

Alyosha   You're becoming bickery in your old age.

Ivan   Hey! You ever see *Species II*? You know what happens when you fornicate with a Martian? Because Rose is nearly a Martian now. You fuck her your abdomen will explode!

Alyosha   Ivan. Where is your sense of romance? She's a hero. She's Catherine the Great!

Ivan   She's a long way away.

Alyosha   Why are you leering at me?

Ivan   You know where we're going?

Alyosha   No.

Ivan   Road movie!

Alyosha   What?

Ivan   That's all they're doing. You know, the old days, sailor sets out scared shitless of dragons and sirens and tsunamis. Now it's solar flares, cosmic radiation. We don't have a galleon. But we have my car.

Alyosha   It must be a piece of junk.

Ivan   It's a Lada Sputnik 1.3. Russian junk. Not your generalised motors.

Lying down.

Ivan   We're going to Kolyma.

Alyosha   What?!

Ivan   In Siberia.

Alyosha   Yes, I'm aware of the location of Kolyma.

Ivan   So?

Alyosha   So it's Gulag, Ivan. You want to drive two thousand miles to a death camp in the middle of nowhere. Why?

/

Ivan   Because he was there.

Alyosha   It's the middle of the winter, Ivan.

Ivan   And it's important.

Alyosha   Why?

Ivan   I don't know yet.

Lights change.

Transition

Transition tone begins.

The **Brothers** *stand and begin to move the portals into new positions.*

They talk to each other and crucially to the audience.

Ivan   This is the beginning of our journey together.

Alyosha   Two thousand one hundred and twenty-five miles in total. From Moscow to the eastern edge of Siberia. Well. That was our plan.

Ivan   The drive to start a journey with someone can take many forms. But the best journeys are the unexpected ones. The ones that start at three a.m. over a vodka bottle by the Kremlin wall. At this moment I didn't really know what we would find. But I knew this was the last time I could travel with my brother before I lost him to America completely.

Imke *walks on from stage right with a galleon on a table.*

Ivan *brings Mars model back into the space and begins to manipulate it again, by taking things out of his bag.*

Alyosha   So that's what we did. We filled the tank and off we went. At three a.m. in the middle of a Russian winter. Fuelled by –

Ivan   – Alyosha!

Alyosha   Well, I guess I was following my older brother.

Jun *arrives in the space with* **Imke**. *Their theme begins.*

Scene Five
IMKE/JUN 2

Imke *is in the Recreational HAB, working on a model galleon.*

Jun *looks at a plan on the floor, up at the galleon, back at the plan, and at the galleon again.*

Jun   The picture on the box looks somewhat . . . different. Is it meant to be an identical match?

Imke   It's the sails . . . they're fiddly.

Jun   Would you like to see the instructions?

Imke   That's cheating. I used to make models with my father, and he always said, 'If you can't make something by seeing the parts separately, you shouldn't be making it in the first place.'

Jun   That's an interesting theory.

Imke   When Shari said we needed to bring something from home, it just made sense to bring a galleon. The Dutch were great sailors, Jun.

Jun   I read that in my database. 'The Dutch were great sailors.'

Imke   I just need Oskar to hold the mast while I glue the sails.

Jun   Oskar does have excellent dexterity –

Imke   He does.

Jun   – and above average analytical skills.

Imke   Steady on, Jun, he's taken.

Jun   However, Oskar does have his own recreational activities, Imke.

Imke   Where is Oskar?

Jun   Oskar is clearing dust from the solar panels.

Imke   Still? Can you send a message out to the rover telling him to hurry up? He said he would help me in the nursery three hours ago. I want to send Shari an update on the plants by the end of the day.

Jun   I'm sorry that your botany research isn't progressing as quickly as you'd hoped. You and Oskar have a scheduled drilling session tomorrow, Imke. Perhaps you will find something helpful in the Martian soil.

Imke   Perhaps.

Jun   Should I leave you alone, Imke?

Imke   No. I shouldn't let my research frustrate me.

Jun   Cultivating vegetation in this environment is a difficult task, Imke. You must not forget how important your research is for the future of humankind on Mars.

Imke   That's a big thought for the morning, Jun.

Jun   OK, Imke.

Imke *pats* **Jun** *affectionately.*

Imke   It's a good thought to hold on to though. Thank you.

Transition

Ivan *and* **Alyosha** *are stage right.*

Techno music can be heard as if in the distance, from a club on top of a skyscraper, gradually becoming louder and louder as the **Brothers** *set the scene. Music thumps.*

Shari *and* **Rudi** *enter in slow motion – they are both having drinks in a nightclub.*

Alyosha   Meanwhile, fifty-six million kilometres away in a nightclub in Chennai –

Ivan   – Shari and Rudi are celebrating the fact that Ghara is on its final approach to Mars Orbit.

Scene Six
SHARI AND RUDI'S NIGHTCLUB/TAKEAWAY JOINT

Behind them the 2001: A Space Odyssey *video is playing.*

We see the surtitles of what they're saying.

Rudi *isn't as drunk as* **Shari***.*

The music kicks in and the slow motion turns into terrible, uncontrolled dancing. The sort of dancing you see academics attempt on a night out.

Alyosha *and* **Ivan** *have become* **Shari***'s security staff by putting on a pair of dark glasses.*

Rudi   They follow you everywhere!

Shari   Extra security.

/

Rudi   I haven't been to a club in *years*!

Shari   What, you're trendy!

Rudi   Haha!

Shari   You did very well today.

Rudi   Thank you, madam.

Shari   No, seriously, you deserve the promotion. You've been doing some great work since the launch.

Rudi   What exactly happened with Nikolai?

Shari   It wasn't really working out.

They step forward to another space and the sound drops down in volume.

Rudi   How come?

Shari   He kept making mistakes.

Rudi   High-pressure environment.

Shari   Not my problem. It's great to have you on board.

Rudi   They're nearly in Mars Orbit now. It's . . . well, it's amazing.

Shari   Completely mind-boggling.

Rudi   What?

Shari   It's mind-boggling. They've travelled fifty-six million kilometres across our solar system.

Rudi   You sound surprised.

Shari   No no. It's just . . . when you stop and think about it. It's completely –

Rudi   – mind-boggling

They both laugh. Almost uncontrollably.

Shari   What *is* this music?

Rudi   Dunno. You're into classical, right?

Shari   Yeah. The Germans and the Russians.

Rudi   What?

Shari   The Germans and the Russians are the true masters.

Rudi   Yeah, like Wagner, right?

Shari   Wagner, Rheinberger, Shostakovich. Choral music is the best though. It's my dream to fill a cricket stadium and hear eighty thousand sopranos, altos, tenors and basses sing 'Abendleid' by Rheinberger. Waaaaah!

Rudi   Yeah yeah yeah, I've heard you listen to that. You turn it up loud in the morning and evening.

Shari   Dawn and dusk.

Rudi   What?

Shari   Beginning and end.

Rudi   Right?

Shari   The cleaners.

Rudi   What?

Shari   It blocks out the noise of the vacuums. I can't stand vacuums. Sounds like there's a bumble bee in my brain, like I'm living inside a nightmare!

Rudi   Haha.

He does a vacuum-cleaner dance.

Shari   You wait. Our offices are next to each other now.

Shari *opens the slide door to the balcony.*

She steps out first, followed by **Rudi**.

The sounds drops.

Shari   Shit. That's so high.

Rudi   Vacuum cleaners and heights?

Shari   When my father visited me at mission control that was the first thing he said: 'You're a bloody flight director and you don't like heights!'

Rudi   You know when Kennedy visited NASA in the early sixties, he bumped into a cleaner in the corridor on his way to the flight deck, knocking her over. And he said, whilst picking her up – (*Acting this out.*) 'Oh I'm sorry, ma'am. What do you do here at NASA?' And you know how she responded? How the cleaner responded?

Shari   Yeah, I heard this somewhe –

Rudi   – She said: 'Oh good morning, Mr. President. I'm just helping to put a man / on the moon.'

Shari   On the moon, yeah. You weren't a twinkle in your mother's eye when they landed on the moon.

Rudi   Doesn't make it any less special.

Shari   Very true.

Rudi *opens the slide door and heads back inside, leaving* **Shari** *outside. She looks at her watch, realises it's just gone midnight and bursts back into the club after* **Rudi**.

Shari   Hey – it's my birthday.

Rudi   What?

She considers for a moment that she's let her guard down.

Shari   I said . . . I said it's a good day.

The sound suddenly drops away.

Ivan *and* **Alyosha** *place a Chinese takeaway carton in* **Rudi***'s lap as* **Shari** *reaches over for more rice.*

Shari *and* **Rudi** *are slumped on the pavement outside a takeaway joint. Flickering neon lights can be seen.*

Shari   I mean what is it with the cap-coms guys? It's like they're the cowboys of the control room.

Rudi   I mean, what do they do? The cap-coms team? What do they actually do? They read from a transcript most of the time.

Shari   It's the landings . . . they do step up.

Rudi   Sure. But some of the team need to be told they're not pulling their weight.

/

Shari   We should swap for a day.

Rudi   What?

Shari   You should see what it's like to run the ship.

Rudi   I'd rather stay by your side and learn, madam.

Shari   Good. Because that was Nikolai's problem.

Rudi   Madam?

Shari   He thought he could make decisions without my permission. Total waste of time.

Rudi   It was very sudden. His dismissal.

Shari   Nice boy. But prying.

Rudi   Ma'am?

Shari   You know. I caught him trying to micro-manage my teams. Total waste of time.

Rudi   I'd like to flight direct one day.

Shari   Do as I say, Rudi, and you absolutely will. I promise you that.

Transition

Lights change to the darkness of **Shari***'s office.*

Ivan *and* **Alyosha** *move* **Shari***'s workstation and chair into the space.*

Shari *sits on her office chair and glides backwards.*

Her entire body has gone into freefall.

We hear a recording of **Shari***'s interaction with the Mars One team.*

As she continues to freefall, **Ivan** *and* **Alyosha** *position her into her workstation and we see that she is dreaming.*

The video flickers in the background: the Ghara logo.

There is a sense of **Shari** *dreaming about that fateful night years ago.*

Shari (*voice-over*)   We're now at an altitude of seventy-three miles moving at a speed of 14,942 miles per hour as we enter the Martian atmosphere.

Expected parachute deploy in five seconds.

4, 3, 2, 1 – mark.

We're awaiting confirmation that the parachute has deployed.

Mars One, can you confirm that the parachute has deployed?

Mars One, we're detecting a power loss in the emergency retro-thruster.

Mars One, can you confirm the parachute has deployed?

Alyosha *and* **Ivan** *who have been watching the action, disappear out of the space.*

Shari   No signal at the moment.

Still no signal.

We don't see a signal at the moment.

Scene Seven
SHARI'S OFFICE

Shari's *alarm sounds. This is linked into the sound of an emergency alarm in the previous soundscore.*

Rudi *appears at the doorway, two coffees in his hand. He clocks that* **Shari** *has been here all night.*

He turns on the light. He presses a space bar to stop the alarm. He moves over and opens the blind.

Sound of vacuums next door.

Rudi   Good morning.

Shari (*suddenly jumping awake*)   Oh! My God. My head. I didn't embarrass myself did –

Rudi   – You didn't go home?

Shari   I just needed to finish the –

Rudi   – You should wash your face.

Shari   Those bloody vacuum cleaners. I can wash here.

/

Rudi (*looking on the fourth wall*)   Nice picture.

Shari   You've seen it before. It was my present.

Rudi   From whom?

Shari   On the day of the launch.

Rudi   From Mrs Singh?

/

Shari   Yeah.

Rudi   It's a Roelant Savery, right?

Shari   Yeah, how did you know that?

Rudi   Garden of Eden.

Shari Right.

Rudi My mother loves Dutch art.

/

Rudi You had a call this morning.

Shari From whom?

Rudi The guy hung up before I could take a message.
I traced the number to Kazakhstan.

Shari Oh it was a colleague.

Rudi He didn't leave a name.

Shari We're working on some tech out there.

Rudi I didn't know we had any links in Kazakhstan –

Shari – It's just a bit of blue-sky thinking.

Rudi OK.

/

Rudi Are you coming to watch the broadcast?

Shari God no.

/

Rudi Don't you need to be seen to be there, Shari?

Shari Really?

Rudi Yes, really. I think.

Shari OK.

*The tone of a phone call is coming through **Shari**'s workstation. On the
stage-right space, **Imke** comes in and sits down, holding **Jun**. We see
that **Jun** acts as a video live feed back to earth.*

/

Rudi Shari.

Shari OK.

Shari   Look, I need to pick this up. We go live in ten minutes. right?

Rudi   Sure.

He reluctantly leaves.

Shari *turns the table to stage right.*

Scene Eight
IMKE CALLS INTO SHARI'S OFFICE

Imke   Good morning, Sriharikota, this is Imke wishing you a very happy birthday, Shari!

Shari   You always sound like Eurovision, Imke!

Imke   What?

Shari   Receiving you loud and clear, except for the part about my birthday!

Imke   Twenty-one today.

Shari   Charming.

Imke   It's a good connection today.

Shari   Yes – a very calm sun – not much interference.

Imke   How are things on Earth?

Shari   I'm actually hungover, Imke.

Imke   Shari!

Shari   I know. Don't tell the boss. How is everything in the HAB, Imke?

Imke   Oskar's not back yet.

Through the sound design we hear a distinctive tone, a high pitched drone of suspension.

/

Shari   That's odd.

/

Imke   He should have been back from cleaning the panels twelve hours ago. I can't get through to him via the rover.

Shari   Yes, I can see that.

Imke   I tried to radio him but I couldn't hear anything except white noise.

Shari   How often have you tried?

Imke   Every hour.

Shari   He's been away longer than this before. Probably out of range. I'll try to get him from this end.

Imke   Great.

Shari   Speak soon.

Imke   Shari?

Shari   Yes?

Imke   How did my last broadcast go down?

Alyosha and **Ivan** *are watching* **Shari** *speak. They sit on the edge of one of the portals.*

/

Shari   Very well.

Imke   Good.

Shari   The focus is on the next mission now. They'll be entering Mars Orbit in three days.

Imke   It's going to be amazing to see them.

/

Shari   Yes.

She puts down the call.

Scene Nine

IVAN AND ALYOSHA IN THE LADA SPUTNIK 1.3

Alyosha *and* **Ivan** *are driving across Siberia.*

Ivan *is driving, trying to concentrate while* **Alyosha** *constantly taps on his knees a 5/4 rhythm. This goes on for a little while.*

Ivan   Alyosha. Alyosha, will you cut it out?!

Alyosha   Just go with it, dude.

Ivan   Go with it? Go with this. Shut the fuck up! And don't ever call me dude.

/

Alyosha   Daddy, are we at the death camp yet?

Ivan   Oh my God, it's too early for this. Your tippy-tappy sounds like bullets in my brain.

Alyosha   If you're hung over I should be driving.

Ivan   You can't drive.

Alyosha   You won't let me drive.

Ivan   Because you can't drive. Russian roads are no place to learn.

Alyosha   Oooh, Russia's so big and scary. My name's Ivan and I'm so big and scary and only I may pilot our piece of shit vehicle through . . . Where are we?

Ivan   You serious? We literally just crossed into Siberia.

Alyosha (*phantasmagorical*)   Ooooooh.

Ivan   Are you incapable of taking anything seriously?

Alyosha   I think I might be incapable of taking this seriously, Ivan. Driving across the biggest country in the world in Shitty Shitty Bang Bang with Grumedy Grumpovich from Grumpygrad to visit one of Stalin's most notorious gulags.

Wooo! Happy holidays. Seriously, Ivan, it's a lovely sentiment,
but how long will this take? I have exams in two weeks.

Ivan   It will take as long as it takes. You're worried about
your exams, you can hitch back to Moscow.

Alyosha   Don't be a dick.

Ivan   This guy put men in space.

Alyosha   I knooow.

Ivan   So?

Alyosha   So . . .

Ivan *suddenly gets up and walks forward into the playing space, away
from his younger brother.*

Alyosha   How's Katya?

Ivan   Oh I don't know.

Alyosha   Right.

He gets up and joins his brother.

Ivan   I'm pulling over, let's get a beer.

Alyosha   Woah there. You're hungover –

Ivan   – I'm joking. I want a . . . poached egg.

*A table and two chairs have been rolled on to the stage in front of the
portal.*

Alyosha *and* **Ivan** *take a seat. They are in a rundown roadside diner.*

Ivan *has his handheld camcorder. He is filming his brother.*

Ivan   Haha – this is just like road movies.

Alyosha   What?

Ivan   Like Louise and Thelma.

Alyosha   You ever read Fyodorov?

Ivan   Fyodorov! Why?

Alyosha   Thinking about talking about him in my practical exam. He was the founder of Russian Cosmism.

Ivan   I know. Russian Cosmism, science fiction dressed up as philosophy.

Alyosha   But Fyodorov –

Ivan   – Fyodorov believed that evolution had reached perfection with the human race and we could actually start manipulating evolution itself. He thought that we had a duty to defeat death for ever – to gather every atom of our dead ancestors, even from the far reaches of the universe, and bring them back to life. *And then* of course we had to have somewhere to put all those zombies, so we had to leave Earth, colonise the galaxy, blah blah blah . . .

Fyodorov, little brother, was a nut job.

Alyosha   Then so was Konstantin Tsiolkovsky.

Pause.

Ivan   Tsiolkovsky was a genius. Tsiolkovsky gave us the equation for fuel and acceleration –

Alyosha   – which allowed us to enter into space. But look at this. And you promise not to interrupt?

Ivan   I promise not to interrupt.

Alyosha   OK. So, one day Fyodorov's sat in his library and Tsiolkovsky just walks in the door. He's this weird, skinny, half-deaf kid from the provinces who wants to know what to read next. Fyodorov *sees* something in Tsiolkovsky. He converts him to . . .

Ivan   Russian Cosmism. Hmm.

Alyosha   Now Tsiolkovksy becomes obsessed with the idea that colonising space would lead to the perfection of the human race and that we would become immortal / and that the cosmos is alive.

Ivan   That's ridiculous!

Alyosha   Each atom / of the cosmos is alive, and what's more, sentient.

Ivan   Oh for God's / sake.

Alyosha   It's one unified / consciousness.

Ivan   We've been through this!

Alyosha   And that one day we would learn how to communicate with it.

Ivan   Why would you even want that? What the hell do you discuss with a supernova?

Alyosha   Ivan, don't you see? This isn't some crackpot, this is the guy that made space travel possible! He wrote the equation that allowed Sergei to put the first man in space. The first man on the moon. And now, humans going to Mars. And it had nothing to do with the Cold War or the space race. That little equation was inspired by Russian Cosmism. It came from the belief that our destiny was to attain immortality and become one with the cosmos.

From lunatic to pioneer, in one small step.

A waiter arrives with two cups of coffee

Ivan   Spasiba.

That's . . .

Alyosha   I know.

Ivan   Insane.

Alyosha   I know. So . . . why are we chasing Sergei's memories of a death camp? If we're looking for the birth of space travel, we should see something . . .

Ivan   Insane.

Alyosha   In the 1960s in Novosibirsk some Soviet scientists built a device called the Kozyrev Mirror. Apparently you crawl inside and it blocks off your everyday consciousness and opens your mind up to the universe. You see colours, lights, communicate telepathically. Commune with the cosmos. Where is Novosibirsk?

Ivan   It's like . . . five hundred miles away.

/

Alyosha *smiles.* **Ivan** *realises.*

Ivan   No.

Alyosha   Please.

Ivan   No way. That is a terrible idea. It's pseudo-science.

Alyosha   It's the future, it's a philosophy of space travel.

Ivan   Same thing. It's a terrible idea.

Alyosha   This whole trip was a terrible idea.

Silence. **Ivan** *sighs.*

Ivan   Oh. Fine, we'll go. Watch the camera – I'm going to the little boys' room. And don't steal anything.

Alyosha *waits for* **Ivan** *to leave.*

He looks around and gradually places a few objects from the diner table in his bag as mementos.

Rudi *comes in and pulls* **Alyosha** *out of the space stage left.*

Scene Ten
THE PLANT NURSERY

Imke *and* **Jun***'s theme is playing.*

Imke *is stood to the side of a plant tray where she is trying to nurture seedlings in Martian soil.*

Her eyes are closed.

She can hear crickets. She breathes heavily. The sound of wind and the smell of a beach on earth.

She has some red soil in her hand.

Jun *appears in the doorway.* **Jun** *observes* **Imke** *for a moment and then chooses to gently interrupt* **Imke**'s *ritual.*

Jun   Imke. Imke.

The theme music cuts away and the sound of the habitation module is heard.

Imke   Yes, Jun?

Jun   Are you concerned about Oskar?

/

How does the Martian soil feel?

Imke   Cold.

Jun   It is minus 120 degrees outside.

/

Are you any closer to growing a plant in the Martian soil?

/

You seem upset. Would you like to go into the Nature HAB?

Imke   I don't need the Nature HAB, Jun.

Jun   The Nature HAB is vital to your psychological wellbeing, Imke.

Imke   I know.

/

Jun   How is your algae coming along?

Imke   It won't grow. There's all the same nutrients as Earth. But it's not getting enough CO_2 to develop properly. Why is there so little CO_2?

Jun   The levels are normal for the Martian atmosphere, Imke.

/

Imke   Turn up the UV light from 60 to 80 per cent, please.

Jun   That's too bright, Imke. The algae will not like that.

Imke   I know, Jun. But I don't understand what's wrong with them.

Jun   It's a fragile process, Imke. The spores are perhaps . . . frightened . . . of the Martian soil.

Imke   I'm not sure they're frightened, Jun.

/

Jun   OK, Imke. I'll turn the UV up to 70 per cent. Just for now.

/

Did your drilling reveal anything interesting?

Imke   I'm starting work on the perimeter of our crater tomorrow. But there's nothing here. I'm starting to think the next mission should turn back.

Jun   You're not excited to see them?

Imke   Yes, but I'll have nothing to show them for all my work.

Jun   Perhaps you will find something in the perimeter.

Alyosha *and* **Ivan** *appear in the space. They stand either side of the portal which is the backdrop to the nursery. They gradually glide this portal directly across stage left as* **Imke** *walks, giving the impression that she is moving along a corridor away from the Nursery and towards the Nature HAB.*

Imke   I'm going to the Nature HAB now.

Jun   That's a good idea, Imke.

Part Three

Scene Eleven
THE NATURE HAB I

Imke *is surrounded by video and sound of a waterfall. Throughout this sequence she is able to request that* **Jun** *changes the video and sound at her every command. The overall experience for her is one of immersion. She should have a full sensory experience of her different requests.*

Imke   Change to mountaintop please, Jun.

Jun   In winter or summer?

Imke   Winter.

Jun   OK, Imke. This is the top of the Ural Mountains.

The sound changes.

Imke   Music?

Jun   What music would you like?

Imke   You choose.

Jun   OK, Imke.

/

Bartok's 'Romanian Folk Dances' play.

This is from a square in Amsterdam.

Imke   Princes Canal. I was five years old. How did you know that?

Jun   It's on your memory chart, Imke.

Imke   Turn the volume up.

It does.

Change to rainforest, Jun.

Jun   Which rainforest?

Imke   You choose.

/

Jun   OK, Imke. This is the Borneo rainforest.

Imke   Can you take me into the Amazon instead. I've always wanted to go to the Amazon.

Jun   Of course, Imke.

/

This is Rurrenabache. In the Bolivian rainforest.

Imke *breathes it all in deeply as she curls up inside one of the portals.*

Imke   Can you lift me above the canopy?

It does.

Turn up the sound of the rain slightly.

It does.

Make it greener.

It is.

Make it night-time.

It does.

Show me a camp fire.

It does.

Zoom in on the fire please, Jun.

Jun   OK, Imke.

Imke   Closer . . .

It does.

Imke   Show me some wild life.

It shows fireflies at night-time underneath the fire.

What are they?

Jun   They're *Lampyridae*. Better known as fireflies.

Imke   Something larger.

Jun   OK, Imke.

We see a white rhino in one corner crossing a savana.

Jun   White rhinos went into extinction in 2021.

Imke   Show me something else. From the rainforest.

The fire strip moves away and a boa constrictor appears in the central panel. Above it are fireflies and below is the white rhino.

Jun   Boa constrictors are native to South America.

A boa constrictor appears.

Imke   Pause.

It does.

Zoom in please, Jun.

More.

It does. To its eye.

Alarm sounds. Nature HAB falls away.

Jun   I can detect a solar flare is on its way. We need to get you back into the Protection Hab, Imke.

Imke   Just a little longer?

The stage-right and stage-left portals move with the alarm. Video plays a flashing sign: 'Solar Flare – Warning'.

Jun   I'm sorry, Imke. It's too dangerous to keep you in here. Please return to the Sleeping HAB and step inside the Protection HAB. You have sixty-three seconds before the solar flare arrives.

Scene Twelve
SHARI AND RUDI TALK TO THE ASTRONAUTS

Shari *enters downstage left. She has a headset on as if midway through chatting with* **Gregory**. **Gregory** *is an all-American astronaut.*

Shari   OK thanks, Gregory. We're pleased with your progress back here. You all seem focussed.

Gregory   Yeah, sure thing, Shari.

Shari   You're going live in thirty seconds. I'll hand you over to the media team. Between you and me, I'm sorry about the idiotic questions.

Gregory   Ah, it sounds like you need a good night's sleep, Shari. We're happy to answer whatever the folks back home want to know.

Rudi *enters from downstage right and walks directly across to* **Shari***, who mutes her headset.*

/

Shari   These TV programmes are ridiculous. How do such stupid questions get through?

Rudi   Hey – those are the stupid questions I approved.

Shari   I know. I find it fascinating that people really still want to know what astronauts eat for breakfast or whether they eat their own faeces and drink their own urine.

Rudi   The ratings are breaking records, Shari. We've got the attention of the world. What's wrong?

/

Shari   There's a point of no return. Just before descent. Until that moment they could turn back.

Rudi   I know . . .

Shari   Mrs Singh won't let them descend into the atmosphere unless everything is perfect.

Rudi   What do you mean?

Shari   Everything has to be perfect.

/

Shari   I'll tell you after the broadca –

The Channel 4 'Ghara Landings live' theme interrupts. **Shari** *walks across to downstage right with* **Rudi**. *They watch the broadcast from here.*

Announcer (*voice-over*)   Good evening, folks, and welcome to *Landings Live*.

Dermot (*voice-over*)   Hello, Ghara, this is planet Earth calling.

Rose *is also all-American, from the Deep South.*

Jean-Luc *is French.*

Jean-Luc/Rose/Gregory   Hi . . . Hiya . . . Hi there . . . (*Each a separate response.*)

Gregory   Hi there, Earthlings. We can hear you loud and clear from the flight deck.

Dermot (*voice-over*)   Hello and welcome to *Landings Live*, Commander Adams.

Gregory   Well, thank you, Dermot.

Dermot (*voice-over*)   So we know we don't have you for long. We hear you've just got a strong visual of Mars for the very first time?

At workstations.

Gregory   Ah. Yeah. I can confirm that /

Dermot (*voice-over*)   How does it look?

Gregory   Er . . . Well, Dermot . . . It's er . . . it's awesome.

Rose   Yeah. We can see the Valles Marinaris with the naked eye.

Dermot (*voice-over*)   Hi Jean-Luc, it's good to see you. So, I'm going to go ahead here and ask some questions which have come through 'group media' here on Earth.

Jean-Luc   Yes, great.

Dermot (*voice-over*)   We have a question here from, Clair, aged seven, from Toulouse. She wants to know what you had for breakfast today?

Shari   Jesus Christ. I'm going to get some air.

Rudi   Good idea.

Shari   Fine.

She leaves across to stage left.

Jean-Luc   I wish I could say fresh omelette but things are a little more synthetic for us.

Dermot (*voice-over*)   And a question for you, Rose, from David Smith in Boston, USA. He wants to know what the health risks are for you all up there?

Rudi   Well, arggh . . . that's quite a complicated question to answer, Dermot. But . . . well . . . we had a solar flare come in this morning . . . We have a room which we can go to at heart of our living quarters . . . We all hunker down in there if, er . . . one comes along. It's very safe in there and protects our bodies from radiation.

Dermot (*voice-over*)   That must be good to know. And finally, Gregory, a question for you, Akram in Edinburgh. He wants to know how often you get to speak to your family back home?

Gregory   Hey there, Akram. Er, thanks for your question. Um. Well. I personally try not think about home too much. But you know, er, we try to touch in every few days. Rose and I have some photos of our family and friends in our living quarters . . . But you know the work schedule up here is pretty constant . . . but we do what we can to keep connected with what's going on back on terra firma.

Transition

A large piece of classical music plays.

Rudi *walks in slow motion from stage right to stage left in a corridor of light. This is a homage to the airplane scene in* 2001: A Space Odyssey.

The two portals glide back into position of the Nature HAB.

We see **Imke** *curled up in the central portal, clearly showing the signs of distress.*

Scene Thirteen
NATURE HAB 2

The Nature HAB plays old black-and-white movies, an attempt to help **Imke** *feel normal.*

Imke   Has the rover found anything, Jun?

Jun   Try to relax, Imke. The Nature HAB is designed to deter psychological distress.

Imke   He will be running out of core oxygen by now.

Jun   Oskar will have around 32 per cent oxygen remaining depending on how active he is. He has emergency oxygen too.

/

It's possible he has simply lost communication with our HAB and that all is well.

Imke   Increase colour saturation.

It does.

Imke   More.

It does.

Jun   Are you sure, Imke? It's not a very realistic representation.

/

Alyosha *and* **Ivan** *enter the space. They begin to rotate the portal on the spot. This gradually increases in speed during the scene until we only see glimpses of* **Imke**.

Imke   Show me a live volcano then.

It does.

Jun   This is not very calming for you, Imke.

Imke   Cut music.

It does.

Bird's-eye view please, Jun.

Zoom in.

/

Imke   Jun. Zoom in.

Jun   Your heart rate has increased to 103 bpm. I'm worried about you, Imke. Perhaps we should leave the Nature HAB for now.

Imke   Jun, zoom in.

Jun   That's not advisable, Imke.

/

Imke   Show me objects falling then.

Flocks of geese flying, swooping down, quiet wind.

Not that. Show me things breaking.

/

It shows objects, buildings being destroyed.

Put that on repeat.

Increase the volume.

It does.

Louder

It does.

Louder!

Jun   Imke, you appear to be distressed. May I suggest you select something more calming?

/

Imke   Jun, can you show me Oskar please.

All sound and video falls away. Only silent white space projected. This is a vast contrast.

Jun?

Jun   I've been advised not to do that.

Imke   Who told you not to do that?

*She stands up and out of the portal, which then travels backwards in the space, leaving **Imke** fragile in the middle of the Nature HAB.*

Jun   I've been advised not to show you images of Oskar.

Imke   Override that setting.

/

Jun   I can't do that.

Imke   Jun, I need to see Oskar.

/

Jun   OK, Imke. What would you like to see?

Imke   I want to see his eyes. Bring them into focus please, Jun.

Jun   I can try, Imke.

Imke*'s theme begins.*

Jun   Wait a moment please.

/

Imke   Show me some moving images of him. He can't have just disappeared, prepare my suit.

Jun   We will find him, Imke. He can't be far away.

/

Imke   What do you mean, 'He can't be far way'?

/

Jun   I'm trying to be empathetic, Imke. I'm worried about him and I'm worried about you.

Imke   Why hasn't Shari been in touch?

The high-pitched drone can be heard again.

/

Jun   Shari is looking for him, Imke. Oskar's behaviour is irrational.

Imke   You've become more formal with me, Jun. Why have you become more proper with me?

/

Jun   I'm concerned for you, Imke.

Imke   Leave now, Jun.

Jun *does so.*

Imke   Oskar. Where did you go? Talk to me, Oskar.

She leaves the Nature HAB.

Part Four

Scene Fourteen
SHARI AND RUDI MOVING THROUGH CORRIDORS

A long corridor of light appears spanning from stage right to stage left.

A thumping beat is heard. It is the beginning of the corridor music.

Shari *bursts into the corridor from downstage left and travels down the corridor with* **Rudi** *in pursuit.*

During this scene the portals glide across the playing space to create different doorways, turnings in corridors and a lift.

Imke *and* **Jun** *operate one portal.* **Alyosha** *and* **Ivan** *operate the other.*

Generally **Rudi** *is in pursuit of* **Shari**, *who gradually confides in him.*

Rudi   I got your message. You sounded sweaty.

Shari   What?

Rudi   You sounded like you were sweating. Talk to me.

Shari   It's bloody boiling in here.

Rudi   It's normal temperature. How can I help?

Shari   I don't know.

Rudi   Shari?

Shari   What?

They stop. **Shari** *walks off.*

Rudi   Shari?

Shari   Yes.

Rudi   You asked me to come and help you.

Shari   I need to figure something out. It's Imke.

/

Rudi   Is this . . . ? Are we talking about this here? Shari –

Shari   – Oskar is not coming back and Imke wants to go and look for him.

Rudi   Right . . .

Shari   But we need to keep on track, don't we?

Rudi   Yes, of course, so we need to make sure Oskar –

Shari   Oskar will be fine. Imke must stay inside until we're ready to bring her out.

Rudi   Shari!

They step into the lift.

Shari   Look, when I let you into this you promised me you'd do anything to help. Right?

Imke is looking for someone to blame for Oskar's disappearance.

Rudi   She doesn't trust you any more.

Shari   That's not what I said.

Rudi   Shari, that's what it sounds like.

Shari   OK.

Rudi   So who does she trust?

Shari   Her sister, Maartje.

The artificial sound of the lift arriving at the seventh floor and the doors opening. The two bodyguards, played by **Aloysha** *and* **Ivan** *get into the lift.* **Ivan** *presses the button.*

Shari   Hello, boys.

They all stand in an awkward silence for a moment and the lift travels up.

It pings. The bodyguards get out. The doors shut. **Shari** *hits the button to continue.*

Rudi Right.

Shari There's not a hope in hell Maartje would talk to me.

Rudi Have you tried?

Shari No.

Rudi Why not?

Shari I need your help.

Rudi With getting hold of her. You need me to cover for why there's an unnamed civilian coming into mission control.

Shari No – Mrs Singh can't know about this. She can't know I'm losing control of this –

Rudi – Shari, you're asking me to lie to Mrs Singh.

Shari Will you help me or not?

/

Rudi Where is Maartje?

Shari She's in the middle of the Pacific.

From stage right, **Alyosha** *and* **Ivan** *are moving a portal in front of this scene which is playing out.* **Imke** *is on a top bunk inside the portal.*

Rudi What?

Shari She's a marine biologist.

Rudi Will Imke speak to her?

Shari Either way, we're running out of time. We need to be careful, we don't know how she's going to react.

The sound of the lift pings. **Shari** *and* **Rudi** *step out of the back of the lift.*

Scene Fifteen
BLACKOUT

Imke *is on the top bunk.*

Imke   Why have you locked the door to the HAB?

Jun   You have a high fever, Imke, you should keep inside your bunk.

Imke   I'm manually de-wiring the emergency and UV lights to save power.

If I don't save power, the solar panels will stop purifying the air.

Jun   You really should go and rest.

Imke   You know something strange? In my soil samples I discovered something extraordinary. I saw under the microscope what looked like fossilised bacteria. Do you know what that means, Jun?

Jun   I do, Imke.

That is an extraordinary discovery. You really should contact Shari right away.

Imke   I'm not going to tell her.

Jun   But Shari would really like to hear that news, Imke.

The strange tone can be heard.

Imke   Last night I got up to look out of the portal in the middle of the night.

She is looking out of the portal.

And as I looked out I swea . . . I swear I saw a silhouette hover across the sky. And you know another thing, I swear I heard the sound of a bird calling out.

Jun   You have begun to mildly hallucinate, Imke. The pitch and tone of the air purifier shares many tones with airborne wildlife.

Sound of the HAB powering down at source.

Jun   It's not advisable to turn off the power at source, Imke. I'm sorry I can't do more to help.

Rudi and **Shari** *move the portal to upstage right and then slot it in behind the current position.*

Scene Sixteen
IVAN AND ALYOSHA ARRIVE AT THE GATES OF THE KOSREYEV MIRRORS

Alyosha *rushes through the portals as if through a long tunnel, followed slowly by* **Ivan**, *who is eating a lollipop.*

The sun is shining brightly.

Alyosha *sees a 'Closed' sign and is obviously distraught and then reads out aloud.*

Alyosha   'Kosreyev Mirrors . . . Closed'.

Ivan   Well . . . at least they've put a sign up.

Alyosha   This fucking country.

I couldn't have known they'd closed d −

The page said . . . You don't believe me.

Ivan   OK.

Alyosha   What?

Ivan   OK.

Pause. He crunches the lollipop

Well at least we now know what's it like to be cosmonauts.

You travel a long long long way . . . and there's fuck-all there when you arrive.

Would you like to return to planet Earth now, little brother?

Alyosha *is near to tears.*

Ivan   What did you expect?

Alyosha   I don't know.

/

How long do you think it's been closed?

Ivan   The place looks like a shell. A while I'd say.

So much for the future, Alyosha!

Nice detour.

Alyosha   Don't even –

Ivan   – I'm kidding. We could always go and see a rocket launch?

Alyosha   What?

Ivan   We're not actually that far from Kazakhstan.

Alyosha   Not far?

Ivan   Well, not far in Russian terms. A day's drive, maybe two. And the Baikonur Cosmodrome is in Kazakhstan. It's where Sergei conducted most of his experiments. It's where Gagarin launched from. It's still operational. Unlike your mirrors.

Alyosha   Where exactly?

Ivan   Details, Alyosha, details. It's somewhere in Kazakhstan.

Alyosha   Kazakhstan is a pretty big place –

Ivan   – It's somewhere in Kazakhstan! We'll find it.

Maartje *enters downstage right. She is dressed in smart, navy-blue clothing.* **Aloysha** *switches into narration mode.*

Alyosha   This is Maartje. Imke's sister. They haven't spoken since the day of the launch.

Rudi, **Shari**, **Ivan** *and* **Imke** *rotate the three portals, now in a cube. They rotate the cube clockwise until the bunk bed is facing downstage, giving* **Maartje** *a workstation inside her deep ocean submarine.*

Part Five

Scene Seventeen
DEEP SEA SUBMARINE

Video of ocean hydrothermal vents.

Sound of water-pressure gauges, robotic arms and deep ocean currents.

On the downstage right table we see **Richard**, *a young Australian navigator, lean into the microphone to speak to* **Maartje**.

Richard   Er. We're at a depth of . . . six miles, 352 feet and counting, Maartje. Water pressure 16,000 psi. Outside temperature . . . 0.23 degrees centigrade, visibility 13 mil.

Maartje   Yeah, OK, thank you, Richard, that's fine . . .

Sound of an air stream burst . . .

Richard   Woah . . . what was that?

Maartje   Just a rip-current. OK, we're approaching our final depth. We've nearly made it to the Pacific plain.

Richard   That's great news, Maartje. How does it feel to be at the bottom of the world?

Maartje   Strangely relieved!

Richard   OK, that's great news. Keep her steady. Take the first sample.

Maartje   Yep, will do. OK, sending in the robotic arm . . . now.

Pause.

God. Look at that. Nothing.

Richard   OK. Move along the northern ridge. Take it easy. We're uncharted here.

Alyosha, *who has been playing* **Richard**, *joins* **Ivan** *to narrate.*

Ivan   Staring up and out through the nine-inch-thick porthole, she is struck by the insanity of travelling to this remote place. At the bottom of the Pacific Ocean it is far from the world of sunlight and air that a human could voyage. She looks out and realises that this place has never before been seen by human eyes. And as she stares out –

Alyosha   – she sees something. Like a bird hovering on a thermal wind on one of the monitors. At first, it isn't clear. But then something in her brain tells her to progress.

Alyosha *returns to playing* **Richard**.

Maartje   OK. Zoom in on that.

Richard   Er . . . Is that OK?

Maartje   No. A little closer.

Richard   What is that?

Maartje   It's a hydrothermal vent.

Richard   OK.

Maartje   Taking a sample now. Putting it under the microscope.

Ivan   And as she travels across this darkling plain, she realises that nature's imagination is so much more instinctive than our own and that nature's ability to re-invent its own rules is seemingly boundless. And maybe that's what she is really here to witness. From lunatic to pioneer in one small step.

Maartje   Richard . . . It's . . . it's incredible. It's some kind of spherical bacteria. I've never seen anything like it. They're different sizes –

Richard   – Wow. Yeah, we're getting images up here too. Let's see if this really is non-carbon life here. Our very own alien life forms.

Maartje   Yes. Yes. Let's go a little furth –

Richard   – Er, Maartje? The captain here says there's a helicopter on approach for you. He sounded pretty serious.

Maartje   What? No, Hang on.

Richard   Yeah, we're going to have to start bringing you up now. I'm sorry, Maartje, if there was anything I could do I would you know –

We hear the approach of a helicopter which loudly breaks the space.

Two portals are manoeuvred into stage-right and stage-left positions.

Imke *enters with a suitcase and thrusts it into* **Maartje***'s hand as she gets into a portal, which has transformed into the passenger hold of a Chinook helicopter.*

The helicopter gets very loud and we hear the following conversation over a radio.

Scene Eighteen
HELICOPTER

Bret *is an American pilot. He's very positive, which is the antithesis of* **Maartje***'s fury.*

Bret   Morning. ma'am. Have you got your belt on?

Maartje   What?

Bret   Your belt. Have you got it on properly?

Maartje   Yes. I've got my belt on. Is this to do with the latest samples? Are we going to the mainland?

Bret   I'm not allowed to talk details I'm afraid, ma'am.

Maartje   Never in my entire career have I been treated this way. It's an embarrassment.

Bret   All will be explained later.

Maartje   I'm in the middle of a very important study, with twelve members of staff and head office decides to call me away. Never in my entire career.

Bret   I don't work for head office.

Maartje   Well, I'm telling you now this will not go down well.

Bret   Everything will be explained.

Maartje   I'm telling you now this will not sit well.

/

What do you mean, you don't work for head office?

Bret   I work for an independent company.

Maartje   What?

Bret   I said I work for an independent company.

Maartje   Then who exactly do you –

Bret   – I can't talk details, I'm afraid.

/

Maartje   Why are we travelling east? You're going the wrong way.

Bret   We're heading to LA.

Maartje   LA? We're heading for LA?

Bret   Yes.

Maartje   And what the hell is in LA?

Bret   The airport.

Maartje   The airport?

Bret   You're getting on a flight. To India. You'll be flying to India from there.

Maartje   India? You're wearing a Ghara badge.

/

Bret   I'm not meant to be disclosing details, ma'am.

Maartje   Yeah – well, you're doing very well at that.

Maartje *steps out of the portal.*

The soundscape changes to an airport as she stands in a narrow corridor of light.

We hear the following announcement at LAX.

Announcement (*voice-over*)   This is the final call for Air India Flight 346 to Kolkata. Please make your way to Gate 7.

We see **Shari** *glide into her workstation from stage left.*

Scene Nineteen
IMKE LEAVING A MESSAGE FOR SHARI

Shari *watches the screen at her workstation. She is concerned.*

We see **Alyosha** *holding* **Jun** *over* **Imke***, who is lying on the bunk bed in the upstage-right portal. This is a live feed of her face.*

Imke *has left* **Shari** *a message explaining how she feels about* **Oskar***'s disappearance.*

Imke*'s theme is playing. As if her heartbeat is slowly slowing down.*

Imke   My eyes feel like they're on fire.

I can't sleep, Shari. I've started . . . I've started to see things.

I keep thinking I hear the airlock open. But it doesn't. I keep thinking I've seen his face in the portal but he isn't there.

The stupid thing is I know what's happening to me. It's the oxygen levels. They're down to 15 per cent. But there's nothing more I can do to save power. Except turn Jun off.

/

You won't let me leave the HAB and you won't explain why.

I've gone over every possibility and it doesn't make sense.

I don't trust you any more.

So I'm not going to respond to your messages, Shari.

I discovered something in the soil yesterday. I found bacteria. The sort which might have lived at the bottom of an ocean.

/

Maartje *slowly walks along the corridor from stage right to stage left.*

Imke   I've shut down the computer systems to save power until I work out what to do.

I'm keeping Jun on for now.

Scene Twenty
MAARTJE AND SHARI

Maartje *appears in the doorway. She watches* **Shari** *at her workstation for a moment.*

Maartje   Hello, Shari.

Shari   Hello, Maartje. I suppose you're wondering –

Maartje   – What I'm doing here? Yes, actually.

You fly me to India, when the last time I saw you we were in Kazakhstan. You . . . you ignore my calls, you don't allow me to speak to my sister, even though you promised I would be able to. You tell me she's going to broadcast to the world and no one even knows she's up there –

Shari   – Thank you for coming.

Maartje   I didn't have much choice. I was pulled out of a study.

Shari   Please, Maartje.

Maartje   One of the most important moments of my career actua –

Shari   – which Mrs Singh helped to fund.

/

Maartje   Why am I here?

Shari   Oskar's missing. He's been gone four days. Imke's not coping well. Jun tells us she's beginning to hallucinate, that she's experiencing psychological trauma.

/

Look, Maartje. I need you to communicate with her. I need you to tell her to hold on until the next landings. To stay inside the HAB for her own safety.

/

I've been trying to communicate with her but she doesn't trust me any more.

Maartje   Good!

Shari   Please, Maartje.

Maartje   Please what?

Shari   For the sake of your sister you need to help us.

Maartje   This is bullshit.

Shari   Can you hear yourself?

Maartje   I can't believe I'm here –

Shari   – For Imke's sake –

Maartje   – listening to your lies.

Shari   I'm not lying to you.

Maartje   Two years I've been trying to contact you, Shari. Two years! And now you need my help?

You've got gall.

Don't contact me again. I mean it this time.

Alyosha and **Ivan** *have climbed on top of the stage-right portal.*

Part Six

Scene Twenty-One
THE BROTHERS WAIT FOR A NIGHT LAUNCH

The **Brothers** *lie watching a desert night sky. They are waiting for the launch.*

Ivan   Trust me. It'll be worth it.

Alyosha   It's cold enough to freeze hell out here.

Ivan   Two more minutes. The night launch is scheduled for three a.m. then we can drive on.

Alyosha   Fine.

/

What's up? You seem really distant.

Ivan   What do you mean? I'm here, aren't I?

Alyosha   You're here but you're not here.

Ivan   No, I'm here and here and fucking here. On top of my car. With you.

Alyosha   She's still warm.

Ivan   What?

Alyosha   From the sun.

Pause.

Ivan?

Ivan   Thinking.

Alyosha   What are you thinking about?

Ivan   I don't know

Alyosha   How can you not know what you're thinking about?

Ivan (*exasperated*)   Oh my God. Because it doesn't work like that. I'm thinking. Meditating. Orbiting my thoughts, whatever –

Alyosha   – Feels like you're angry with me.

Ivan   I'm not, man, seriously. Stop i –

Alyosha   – Feels like you wish I wasn't here.

Ivan   No.

Alyosha   Well talk to me then.

Ivan   OH MY GOD DO YOU EVER SHUT UP? DO YOU EVER FUCKING SHUT UP?

/

Alyosha   This is exactly why I left.

Ivan   What?

Alyosha   This is why I went to school in the States –

Ivan   – You went to school in the states because Dad had the money. Right. You were in the right place at the right time.

Alyosha   I went because you used to ignore me. You made me feel like shit.

Ivan *shocked, upset.*

Ivan   I didn't ign –

Alyosha   – You did. You ignored me. You always knew best, you always interrupted me, impressing Dad with your big ideas, making me look stupid.

Ivan   Can we not do this now.

Alyosha   When else are we ever going to do it? There couldn't be a better time. We're in the middle of nowhere with nobody here and nothing to do. Why are we doing this again?

Ivan   How can you say that? Does none of this matter to you at all?

Alyosha   Look. You don't have to remind me who our great-grandfather was or what impact he had. I've heard it all my life, it's in every text-book at M.I.T. I know who he was. I know who *I am*.

Ivan   Then where is your respect for the past?

Alyosha   You think I lack respect? Dude, our great-grandfather didn't give a fuck about the past. He was an innovator. He broke his ribs in his training glider because he spent too long looking up out of the cockpit and wondering why he couldn't go higher.

Who survived five months in Kolyma, lost all his teeth and endured endless years fearing execution, and still picked himself up and put a man in space.

And the day after he did that, he looked to the Moon.

You think a man like that ever worried for a single moment that he was going to fail?

He moved forward. Always forward with pride. Where are you moving, Ivan? Huh?

What made you give up? What the hell happened? You know, you were my hero. When we were kids. I worshipped you.

Ivan   Хлопнут без некролога.

Alyosha   what?

Ivan   Хлопнут без некролога. It was his favourite phrase. Roughly translates as 'We will all vanish without a trace'. Be careful how you choose your heroes, little brother.

They can see smoke billowing out from the launch pad and then the blazing light of the cargo rocket as it moves perfectly vertically up into the sky from the horizon.

The **Brothers** *stand and watch. Sound of the night desert and the rush of air.*

Scene Twenty-Two
MAARTJE IN THE AIRPORT CHAPEL

The sound of Rheinberger's 'Abendleid' swells in a distant corner of the chapel.

We see **Maartje** *walk in with her luggage ready to travel back to her research.*

She looks up at the stained-glass window.

She sits on a chair. Takes hold of her crucifix and shuts her eyes.

In the stage-right portal we see **Imke** *lying on the bunk again. She is halluncating.*

On the infinity wall we see footage of **Imke** *happy, back on earth with* **Oskar**.

Scene Twenty-Three
IMKE HALLUCINATIONS I

Almost simultaneously stage right, we see **Imke** *lying on her side inside a portal. The* **Brothers** *stand over her, filming her movements using* **Jun**. *This live feed is projected into the playing space*

Imke (*voice-over*)   It's been days since he left.

I wake and stare at the ceiling of the HAB.

I can feel my body drifting away from me.

Scene Twenty-Four
MAARTJE AND RUDI IN CHAPEL

The focus drifts back to stage left.

Rudi *enters with a bottle of water. He sees* **Maartje** *and then sits with a seat between them.*

He carefully places the bottle of water on the seat between them.

Maartje *opens her eyes. She doesn't acknowledge him as he is a stranger to her.*

He then begins.

Rudi   I've never got over the idea of a chapel in the middle of an airport.

Shari doesn't know I'm here. I think you should know something.

Your sister is on Mars. But she's not 402 million kilometres away.

She's on Shari's version of Mars.

/

Your sister . . . is in a simulation HAB in the Kazakhstani desert.

/

When you watched her launch at the Baikonur Cosmodrome, she was in the rocket.

They both were.

But once in hyper-sleep they were only in orbit around earth for one day.

They re-entered the Earth's atmosphere and touched down in the Kazakhstani desert.

And Jun . . . Well, Jun is just a live microphone and camera and feed from the Cosmodrome.

/

Imke and Oskar are in a preventative secret experiment named 'Pioneer'.

Only a select group of people know why the Mars One mission really failed. They weren't scientists – yes, that was an error – but we overlooked an important part of our hierarchy of needs. The Mars One astronauts didn't have established relationships with one another.

That's why we needed to try to set up an experiment with a couple.

The Pioneer experiment was designed to last two years, at which time the Ghara One mission would be ready to launch.

So Shari told you, told Oskar and Imke everything until the last moment.

It was vital that they believed they were on Mars for the experiment to be good science.

To convince Mrs Singh that couples are the best candidates for one-way missions to Mars.

Just like Gregory and Rose.

But . . . Mrs Singh fell ill eighteen months into the experiment and ordered Ghara One to launch early.

It took me a while to understand why.

And then Shari confided in me.

Maartje   Where . . . where is Oskar?

Rudi   He's currently at the Baikonur Cosmodrome.

/

If Imke stays in the HAB, we might be able to usher her out safely after the Ghara landings. You can trust me.

Maartje   What do I need to do?

The music soars.

Rudi *and* **Maartje** *leave, together with the three chairs.*

Shari *enters stage-left sitting on her chair at her workstation. She is watching the live feed of* **Imke** *slowly deteriorating.*

Scene Twenty-Five
IMKE HALLUCINATIONS 2

Imke (*voice-over*)   Why didn't you come home?

Do you want me to come and find you?

We're running out of time.

Oskar. I miss your warm hands.

Rudi *slowly walks along the corridor from stage right to stage left, aware of what he has just done. He looks over his shoulder, and then confidently walks into* **Shari**'s *office.*

Scene Twenty-Six
GHARA ASTRONAUTS LIVE

Shari   Maartje won't help.

Rudi   What do the psychologists in Kazakhstan say?

Shari   That if Imke leaves the HAB module they'll recommend to Mrs Singh that the landings don't go ahead.

We have to keep her in there, Rudi. Or it's over.

/

Rudi   Maybe Maartje will change her mind.

The Channel 4 'Ghara' theme tune plays again. We're back at the broadcasts.

Rudi *walks across from stage right to stage left to view the broadcast.*

Rose, **Gregory** *and* **Jean-Luc** *are in the central portal.*

Dermot (*voice-over*)   So Rose, can you tell us what it feels like to orbit Mars?

Rose   It feels safe. It's exciting to be nearing the end of our journey.

Gregory   Yeah, it's a different feeling to seeing Earth from the ISS. It's so close.

Dermot (*voice-over*)   For our viewers, the image is so clear because you're orbiting close to the communications satellite. You're looking good, how you feeling?

Gregory   That's right, crystal clear.

Rose   It's nice to see you so clearly.

Jean-Luc   Cautiously optimistic.

Dermot (*voice-over*)   Can you talk us through exactly what's going to happen?

Jean-Luc   The computer does most of the work. It should all go like clockwork.

Rose   We have to strap in. Lots of G-force. We're trying to keep relaxed.

She moves to stage left.

Gregory   Our primary focus is on the moment we enter the Martian atmosphere. We'll have to carry out our landing procedure in a matter of seconds. Six months' travel comes down to a matter of seconds.

Jean-Luc   Like a jumbo jet nose-diving through the sky.

Rose   Which is why we have to keep relaxed and your messages of support have been comforting.

Dermot (*voice-over*)   What's the first thing you have to do when you land?

/

Jean-Luc   Breathe a sigh of relief.

Rose   I'm looking forward to stepping out on Martian soil.

Gregory   I guess we're all looking forward to stepping outside in our suits.

Dermot (*voice-over*)   Have you decided who's stepping out first?

/

Gregory   Well, that's not really our focus right now but, yeah, we've talked about it. We're going to hold hands and step out together.

We hope we'll be in your prayers.

The blind is slowly rolled down in front of the astronauts.

Imke *appears in the stage-right portal.*

She remains lying down.

Scene Twenty-Seven
IMKE HALLUCINATIONS 3

Alyosha *and* **Ivan** *approach* **Jun** *camera. They create the visual effects described in* **Imke**'s *hallucination.*

Shari *continues to watch from her workstation.*

Imke (*voice-over*)   Last night I dreamt I was running through the woods back to my garden gate.

It was sterile.

Except for the smell of a single tulip.

Now I can't push it from my mind.

We see **Maartje** *enter back into mission control and walk down the corriodor towards* **Shari**. *She stops. Prepares herself. And then enters.*

Scene Twenty-Eight
SHARI AND MAARTJE

Shari   Maartje.

Maartje   The cleaner in the corridor asked me what I was doing here. You know what I said?

I said I'm helping my sister to make history.

/

Did she tell you about the night before the launch? Did she tell you that I begged her, I pleaded with her not to go?

Don't leave me on my own. I'm scared. I'm going to be lonely.

Do you know what she said to me? 'We're all mortal, Maartje. We'll return to dust one day. I want to do something important with my life. I want to make a difference.'

We see **Rudi** *walk down the corridor stage right to stage left.*

Maartje   I'm sorry about before. I overreacted. But do you have any idea how hard it is, knowing that your sister is alive when the rest of your friends and family think that she's dead.

Well at least she's leading the way, right?

/

Shari   Thank you for coming back.

Rudi *enters.*

Shari   This is Rudi van der Waal.

Maartje   Nice to meet you.

Shari   He knows about Imke and Oskar. He's working on the landings with me.

Maartje   Today, aren't they?

Rudi   Ten hours.

He exits and walks back down the corridor to the stage-right table.

Maartje *sits at* **Shari***'s workstation and puts an outgoing call to* **Imke**.

Shari *watches from the corner.*

The call rings.

Scene Twenty-Nine
MAARTJA TALKS TO IMKE

Rudi　We're going to send you in live.

Shari　Just try to make her feel safe.

Alyosha *lights up* **Imke** *in the stage-right portal with* **Jun**. **Imke** *picks up.*

Shari　She's picked up.

Maartje　Hello, Imke.

I love you. I hope you've been getting my messages – I've . . . erm . . . I've sent a lot of messages through Shari.

/

They brought me from the Pacific. It's all been very fast. Listen, I don't have much time. They haven't given me much time to . . . talk to you. I need to. I need to say something to you. And you need to listen very carefully.

I've been told that you've started to hallucinate things. And I can imagine you're probably scared. Things aren't what they appear to be and you don't know who to trust. You're beginning to doubt yourself. And perhaps you're tempted to test things out. Explore a little.

Do you remember as children we were always so curious? We used to devour knowledge like we were starving for it. Thousands of books. And of course we had our favourite. The book of Genesis.

You remember what we thought about Eve? What that apple represented for us?

I need you to keep trusting yourself, Imke.

Do you understand what I'm saying?

You need to keep trusting your instincts.

Maartje *looks over to* **Shari**.

Maartje   Shari is lying to you. Get out, get out of the HAB –

Shari *cuts the connection.*

Shari   – That's not what we agreed, Maartje.

Maartje   You can't just cut me off in –

Shari   – Rudi!

Maartje   She's been brainwashed.

Shari   What are you talking about? Rudi!

Rudi *enters.*

Maartje   Put me back on or I'm going to expose this whole thing –

Shari   – You're crazy.

Rudi   Maartje –

Maartje (*to* **Rudi**)   – Did you think I would just lie to her?

Rudi   I don't know what / you're –

Shari   – What does she / mean?

Maartje   Rudi told me everything.

Shari (*to* **Rudi**)   What the hell were you thinking?

Rudi (*to* **Maartje**)   Come with me.

Shari   Fuck. You stupid little –

Maartje   – Let her out.

Shari   It's not as simple as that.

Rudi   Let's go, Maartje.

Maartje   Put me back on.

Shari   No.

Maartje   Then I'm telling everyone.

Shari   If you do that the money's gone. Every cent. Your project in the Pacific is over. You wouldn't dare to –

Maartje   – Try me.

She leaves, running along the corridor stage right to stage left.

Shari   Rudi?

Rudi *follows* **Maartje**.

Shari   Fuck. Oh fuck. You fucking fucking stupid –

In a moment of rage **Shari** *launches her table into the air.*

It is caught by **Alyosha** *and taken out of the space.*

She also picks up and throws a chair into the air. It is caught by **Ivan**, *and taken out of the space.*

Shari *walks out of her office and down the corridor stage right to stage left.*

She is distraught, in floods of tears.

Scene Thirty
THE BROTHERS LEARN TO SPACE TRAVEL

The stage-left portal is revolved to reveal **Alyosha** *and* **Ivan** *in the Lada Sputnik 1.3.* **Alyosha** *is driving.* **Ivan** *is fast asleep on his brother's shoulder.*

The stars are shining.

Alyosha *is distracted, half-looking up at the night sky.*

Alyosha   Ivan. Ivan you're dribbling on me again.

Ivan   Huh? Where are we?

Alyosha   Beside the barren Aral Sea.

Ivan   Still in Kazakhstan.

Alyosha   You fell asleep for too long.

Ivan   Pull over. You can't drive.

Alyosha   It's four in the morning. It's an empty road. I think it's OK, Ivan.

/

You just missed one of those ships. I stopped to film it, look.

Passes over the camera.

You know? The ships which were marooned when they emptied the Aral Sea in the 1960s. Meant to be one of the driest places on Earth now. From a sea to a dry, rocky desert in just over seventy years. Humans, eh? Looks like the surface of Mars now. It's because of all the iron in the soil. It's apparently –

Ivan   – Meant to be hundreds of those ships, out there . . . just . . . rusting away.

Looking up at the sky.

Alyosha   Mars is close.

Ivan   They must be about to land.

He goes to listen in on the radio.

Pause

Alyosha   Trivia. You know what's the closest a human being can come to space travel on Earth?

The closest a human being can come to space travel on Earth is to accelerate to 150 kilometres an hour along a straight desert road in the middle of the night and then switch your headlights off.

Interesting.

They decide between themselves to get to the point of . . .

Ivan   No. No way.

Alyosha   Why not?

Ivan   Pull over, you're like a five-year-old with a machine gun right now.

Alyosha *starts to put his foot down.*

Alyosha   Do it . . . Do it.

Ivan *switches off the light.*

General noise of them grimacing.

Alyosha   OK, that was the test drive.

Ivan   How fast was that?

Alyosha   Eighty.

Ivan   Fuck, that felt faster!

Alyosha   I know. Right? OK

He starts to put his foot down again.

General noise of them grimacing.

Ivan   How fast that time?

Alyosha   Hundred and ten.

They discuss in Russian if they're going to go for it.

Alyosha   Davi?

Ivan   Davi.

Ivan   Proper fucking cosmonauts.

Alyosha   OK. Initialise launch sequence.

Ivan   Brothers killed off.

Alyosha   That's what the audience has been hoping for.

Ivan   Шесть (*six*).

Alyosha   OK, commencing countdown.

Mission control, you seem to have let two complete amateurs into your space rocket.

As the car increases in pace.

Ivan   девять (*ten*), восемь (*eight*), семь (*seven*), Шесть (*six*) . . .

Alyosha   OK.

Ivan   пять (*five*), четыре (*four*), три (*three*) . . .

Ivan/Alyosha   Wooooaaaah.

The **Brothers** *drift downstage in the portal. The lights are switched off. They are travelling through the Cosmos together.*

Part Seven

Scene Thirty-One
HUMANS LAND ON THE SURFACE OF MARS

Rudi *enters stage left and stands in front of the workstation. It is clear that he has taken* **Shari***'s position as she has gone missing.*

We see **Shari** *climb on top of the stage-left portal and begin to walk stage left to stage right. She is on top of a skyscraper, contemplating jumping.*

We see a video animation of the Mars landing procedure projected on to stage-right and stage-left portal.

We hear this as if over a radio.

Rudi (*voice-over*)　We have just passed one minute to atmospheric entry. Current altitude 121 miles. Current velocity 12,084 miles per hour.

Movement sequence.

We are now at an altitude of 73 miles. Moving at a speed of 12,192 miles per hour. Expected parachute deploy in . . . five seconds.

4, 3, 2, 1 mark. We're awaiting confirmation that the parachute has deployed.

Mission Control (*voice-over*)　Parachute has been detected.

Gregory (*voice-over*)　Heat shield deploy demand.

Rudi (*voice-over*)　Er . . . spacecraft reporting that heat shield has been detected.

Gregory (*voice-over*)　Lander has engaged.

Rudi (*voice-over*)　Er . . . spacecraft reporting that lander has engaged. We're reaching our terminal velocity.

Spectral rocket on my mark . . . Mark.

Shari *throws herself off the portal, to her death.*

Rudi (*voice-over*)   At this point in time we should be on the ground . . .

Any signal that we receive from now indicates that the vehicle would be alive on the ground and bouncing. The spacecraft has to survive all the bounces for the landing to be a success.

No signal at the moment.

Stand by.

Signal strength is currently intermittent.

We don't see a signal at the moment.

We see it.

We see it.

General noise of celebration at mission control. **Rudi** *remains calm.*

Rudi   We've got the signal.

Gregory. What can you see?

Gregory (*voice-over*)   We had some words prepared but we are speechless up here . . . it feels good to have our feet back on solid ground. Gosh . . . it's so quiet . . . and weirdly beautiful. Yeah.

Rudi *leaves with the workstation stage left.*

The stage-right and stage-left portals fold into the centre of the space to create a triangle.

The three portals are lit from the inside, creating a glowing effect.

Imke *is inside the triangle as it rotates around her.*

She is in the decompression chamber preparing to leave the HAB.

Scene Thirty-Two
IMKE LEAVES THE HAB

The music surges.

We see a Ghara mission psychological analyst sitting at her desk. It is **Jun***. She sits with a clip board and a microphone, and is responding to* **Imke**.

The music falls away.

Imke   Jun.

Jun   Yes, Imke.

Imke   I'm gong to turn you off now so you won't be alone.

Jun   Where are you going, Imke?

Imke   I'm going to find Oskar. I need to bring him home.

Jun   But your viewers and Shari will be disappointed.

Imke   I spoke to Maartje. Shari has been hiding something from me.

Jun   Shari is trying to protect you, Imke. She's trying to keep you safe.

Imke   There's something I need to tell you, Jun.

During this sequence all characters enter the triangle and gradually dress **Imke** *into her spacesuit.*

Scene Thirty-Three
FINALE

The structures begin to move. She is putting on her suit.

Imke (*voice-over*)   They say your life on Earth has ended when you go to Mars.

A one-way trip to another world.

Shari told us that our mission would be a secret until we actually landed and that, once on Mars, our success would be broadcast to the world. But it wasn't fame I was searching for.

When we were approached, Oskar refused and threatened to expose the whole project. But I was fascinated.

She leaves the HAB. We hear her breathing.

The three portals rotate. **Imke** *is climbing down the ladder and onto the Martian soil.*

Imke (*voice-over*)   My sister and I always dreamt of exploring. That's what she does now. She takes herself to the bottom of our oceans, looking for life. Looking for something which will change the world.

I wanted to do the same.

Oskar . . . well, Oskar was not happy. But he wanted to stay with me so . . . he agreed.

And so we told one person, Maartje.

She agreed to be part of our pseudocide.

It's a word I wasn't familiar with.

The portals open up from the triangle again into one long line from stage right to stage left.

Imke *is standing alone on the Martian soil.*

Imke (*voice-over*)   Faking our death was an extreme but nonetheless important way of disappearing us from the world.

We created a fiction. Me and Oskar were on a botany research trip in Kamchatka. On the eastern edge of Russia.

And we disappeared. No trace of us.

We went into training in Kazakhstan for a year. And when the day of the launch came. Only Maartje was there.

As they put us up into orbit we saw Earth for the last time.

We stepped into our cooling chambers and knew that six months later, we would wake up on the surface of Mars.

They told us that we would pave the way.

Shari *appears upstage right. She is falling through the air towards the ground.*

Shari (*voice-over*)   Yes, with the help of the Russians, we took them up to orbit.

We put them to sleep for six months.

But they were asleep in a HAB in the Aral Sea basin on Earth.

Outside, a simulation terrain environment one hundred kilometres in diameter.

Exactly the same as the Baykonyr crater in the northern hemisphere of Mars.

Jun rehabilitated them and we began our psychological experiments.

This was what Mrs Singh needed.

She hits the ground.

She needed proof that humans could survive for two years on Mars under significant psychological pressure.

But we told them the truth up until the last moment.

And in that moment. I crossed the line.

We crossed the line. But this is what it is to pioneer.

To see a problem, a possibility, a moment and an opportunity. And I took it.

The **Brothers** *are back in their Lada Sputnik 1.3, the moment before switching off of the lights at 150 km/h to try to space travel. As they do this,* **Rudi** *and* **Shari** *push the portal forwards, swerve and step off the portal to stand above* **Imke***.*

In the middle of the Kazakhstani desert they are standing over an astronaut lying on the floor beside the road.

Imke (*voice-over*)   When the boys found me in the middle of the desert, I was unconscious. I woke up in the back of their car. I'm sure you can image how frightening that was. I thought I was dead.

At first they didn't believe my story but the youngest boy, Aloysha, spoke very good English.

The older, Ivan, was convinced that I should contact the world's media.

Ivan *picks up* **Imke** *and begins to walk upstage and back through the central portal.*

Imke (*voice-over*)   They drove me back to Moscow, where I met with Maartje.

She felt the same as Ivan, but part of me wondered why?

Alyosha *is left looking across the desert night, wondering where she has fallen from.*

Imke (*voice-over*)   Why and how would that help?

Rudi *enters from stage left on his wheelie chair.* **Maartje**, **Imke** *and* **Shari** *follow, entering one by one in a procession, creating a line from stage right to left.*

Rudi   Hello Imke. This is Rudi Van der Waal. I'm sure Maatje has told you about me.

Imke (*voice-over*)   As I flew over the Siberian desert, I got that feeling again, you know. That feeling of how small we are. And then, stepping off the plane in Amsterdam, the winter sun was shining down and I realised that our Earth would fit a thousand times into our star. And that our star, although it is the object which leads our solar system in its great procession, is a mere a dash in the context of our galaxy.

Me and Oskar went through the training.

And apart from a small difference. We were the first to survive on Mars. We were the first couple.

Rudi, the new flight director, contacted me once.

Maatje *enters on a chair.*

Imke (*voice-over*)   He simply said:

Rudi (*voice-over*)   Hello Imke. This is Rudi van Der Waal.

I'm sure Maartje has told you about me.

I'm glad to hear you're settled back in Holland.

It can't have been easy to re-connect with your family and friends.

Imke *enters on a chair.*

Rudi (*voice-over*)   Well . . . I'm getting in touch . . . to thank you. Thank you for your sacrifice.

Old Imke (*voice-over*)   Without us, there wouldn't be colonies on Mars now.

We wouldn't be planning to go to Jupiter's moons.

If I'd exposed my story, the Ghara programme would have been shut down.

Shari *enters.*

Old Imke (*voice-over*)   Perhaps Shari thought that's what I would do.

Perhaps that's why she took her own life.

All begin to rotate on the chairs.

I thought I knew her better than that.

Alyosha *and* **Ivan** *enter from stage right, taking in the others on their chairs.* **Ivan** *moves towards the Mars landscape which has been set downstage left for the show.*

Old Imke (*voice-over*)   I've never had any fame.

And I will die with my secret.

But I know something simple.

And for me it is a simple but important fact.

That I made a difference to the future of humanity.

I was brave.

I still had my Adam and Adam had his Eve.

We had left Eden.

We were pioneers.

Alyosha *and* **Ivan** *are standing over the Martian landscape.*

Video plays a live feed of the landscape.

They slowly bring the structure from stage right to stage left.

Moving with the landscape **Alyosha** *is giving his paper at M.I.T.*

Aloysha   As our solar system was formed there was a moment . . . when the planets clicked into a cosmic procession around the sun.

In this moment . . . Earth and Mars began a particular type of relationship together.

A relationship based upon an ever-changing distance from one another.

At her closest, she is fifty-six million kilometres away. At her furthest, four hundrd and one million kilometres.

So what keeps us connected to our next home?

Our hearts? Our great scientific minds? Our great communicators and philosophers?

Or our ability to go there?

And as we weave a thread backwards and forwards through the future, our relationship will strengthen.

But in that first moment . . .

The landscape arrives downstage right. Back where it began.

Ivan *gathers a chair and moves to a position stage left to create a triangle with* **Imke** *and* **Shari**.

Aloysha   What are we doing?

Are we playing God?

When God formed a man out of the dust of the ground . . . what was he trying to do?

What was it about the dust which drew God in?

In many faiths, the story goes that God was creating a certain type of paradise.

Alyosha *leans in and then moves to stage right to create a triangle with* **Rudi** *and* **Maartje**.

In the two triangle configurations, the three characters rotate three times anti-clockwise, switching positions of chairs. As they do this, they are the next missions after Ghara I. With each new mission, the name of the mission is projected into the space.

Alyosha (*voice-over*)   But what was Eden?

Adam and Eve lived in a simulation, nothing more.

Ghara II, Ghara III.

God created an enclosed area and planted a tree. He planted a seed and waited for human nature to bloom.

Ghara IV.

And Eve. Eve wondered why? She questioned? And when she saw that she was naked, the paradise was broken but not lost.

Ghara V, Ghara VI.

She sacrificed herself because Eve wanted more. She sensed there was surely more to discover. Breaking free, defying restrictions, risking everything and jumping into the darkness.

Ghara VII, Ghara VIII.

It is this darkness where recklessness, where curiosity, where heroism can blossom.

Ghara IX.

This is why humans have survived. This is why we must find a way to call other planets our home.

The two triangles brace as if about to launch.

The music soars. The sound builds to a rocket launch. The light shines.

*The two groups revolve into the middle of the space with **Imke** on a chair, legs up as if floating.*

The characters gather around her and look directly up into a light, as if out of a window looking on to new worlds.

We are on the Callisto I mission.

The sound gradually drifts away, the light gradually fades. We are on our way.

Glossary

Baikonur Cosmodrome   The launch complex where Sputnik 1 and Yuri Gagarin were launched. The town of Baikonur lies 320 km northeast of the complex itself.

Fyodorov (1829–1903)   A Russian Orthodox Christian philosopher and a part of the Russian Cosmism movement. Pioneered radical ideas about space, ocean colonisation and immortality.

Hydrothermal vent   Underwater volcanoes which produce hot springs, first discovered in 1977.

Konstantin Tsiolkovsky (1857–1935)   Russian 'father of rocketry' who developed insights into space travel and rocket science which are still in use today.

Kozyrev Mirror   A device made from aluminium in spiral shapes which are supposed to focus different types of radiation in order to create psycho-physical sensations for the user.

Novosibirsk   Russia's third largest city and the capital of Siberia.

Rolent Savery (1576–1639)   A Flanders-born painter of the Dutch Golden Age.

Rurrenabache   A town in the Bolivian rainforest surrounded by extraordinary scenery.

Russian Cosmism   Existential philosophy that sees the survival of mankind as part of humanity's 'common task', meaning the migration of humans into space is deemed inevitable.

Solar flare   A sudden release of magnetic energy built up in the solar atmosphere causing radiation which spreads across the solar system.

Ural Mountains   A mountain range which forms part of the traditional physiographic boundary between Europe and Asia.

Valles Marinaris   A vast canyon system 4000 km long and 7 km deep running along the Martian equator just east of the Tharsis region.

Above: Shari talks to the world at the launch of Ghara One.
Below: Alyosha searches for his great-grandfather with Ivan.

Above: Jun watches over Imke. Below: Imke lies in the Nature HAB'.

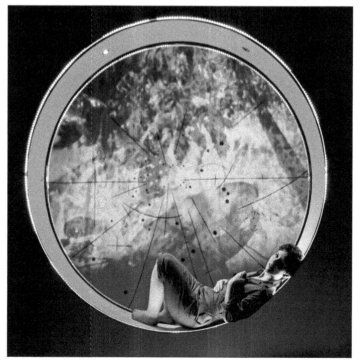

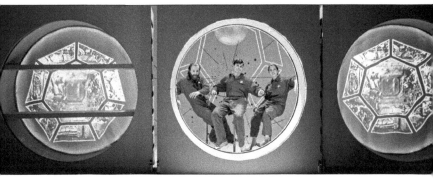

Above: Ghara One astronauts on the flight deck.
Below: Maartje looks out into the deep ocean.

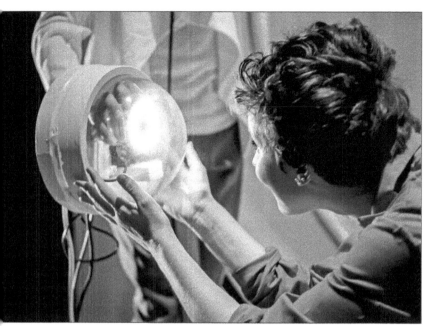

Above: Imke talks with Jun.
Below: Ivan holding the HAB module model landscape.

www.ingramcontent.com/pod-product-compliance
Ingram Content Group UK Ltd.
Pitfield, Milton Keynes, MK11 3LW, UK
UKHW020710280225
455688UK00012B/346

9 781474 255929